Embracing Charlie

March 6th 2017 –

Jarrells Family –

May you find Blessing

recognizing a bit of your

own story in the sharing

of ours! Best, Mindy

MINDY LYNN

ISBN: 150030736X
ISBN 13: 9781500307363

Dedication

For Sophia and Charles
May your trials be slight and fleeting—your blessings abundant. When faced with adversity, may you allow yourself the peace that comes from being held.

Contents

Part I

Embrace, as defined by Merriam-Webster: to clasp in the arms, hug, cherish, love, encircle, or enclose. My favorite: to take up especially readily or gladly (embrace a cause).

Maybe I'm three years old, or perhaps I'm four. I've fallen asleep during an evening car ride home, or maybe I gave in to heavy eyelids as I snuggled up watching TV on the living room couch. It's all the same once I've been scooped up. I'm only slightly roused. My body is limp and heavy. I recognize his scent. It's masculine, but never overpowering. I open my eyes to catch the pattern of his shirt and the soft edge of his collar. Closing my eyes once more, I let my head drape heavily over his shoulder. Part of the magic comes from the sense of floating above the ground. His legs are strong and steady under us. His strength moves us forward. I'm just along for the ride. It's the safest place in the world, the *embrace* of my father. He has taken me up *especially readily* and *gladly*.

Breathless

April, 2005

*I*t was a surreal, life-altering moment—the kind you never forget, the kind that seems so curious you begin to question its legitimacy. Was this really happening? Is this tangible? Here I sat in a wheelchair, in a space that I am certain must have been a storage closet at one time. I imagine it was used to store disinfectants, brooms, and those little plastic peanut-shaped puke buckets. Now, revamped, it looked like a tiny hotel room, complete with muted, natural-hued wallpaper, a TV armoire that doubled as a dresser, and a bedside lamp bolted down to the end table. There was no bed, but in its place was a sofa that housed a teeny pull-out mattress. Unlike any hotel I've ever stayed at, it had a red nurse call button attached to a cord on the wall. Passing down the hallway, you might not notice this hidden place but for the small, inconspicuous sign next to the locked door that said "Parent Sleep Room 1114."

We had been sent here, to room 1114, to wait, ushered away from the commotion of the Neonatal Intensive Care Unit. I had given birth in an entirely different hospital all of an hour ago. Now my mind raced with disjointed thoughts as my arms remained painfully empty at my sides.

What we would learn in the coming weeks is that the Neonatal Intensive Care Unit isn't typically the unnerving scene we had just witnessed. It is, in fact, often quiet and hopeful. Nurses attentively care for teeny, critically ill patients. Parents stay close, often at the side of their child's Isolette, and often in quiet reflection. Doctors hover near. Rooms are dimly lit, and there is a rhythmic, repetitive hum from the multitude of monitors and ventilators.

The noise happens when a baby is in distress and in need of heroic care. Alarm spills in and quickly fills the room. You can see it manifested on the faces of doctors and nurses. The need to preserve life pushes them forward. They work through the shallowness of their own breath, waiting to exhale until life is stable once more.

The pressure is heightened beyond that of other emergencies. These are babies after all, most of whom are premature. They are tiny beyond imagination. They have yet to know life, the palpable kind which grips beyond these walls. Everything that happens here is to offer a chance at that palpable, gripping life experience. It's about pastel balloons, "Welcome Home" banners, and teddy bears. The stakes are exceptionally high.

We waited. An IV still pierced my hand, and the effects of my epidural still lingered in my legs. My husband, Paul, was slow to give details, only offering a sentence at a time. He sensed my fragility. My mother and a nurse who had been sent with me from the adjacent hospital sat quietly beside me.

I had given Paul an assignment. Immediately following the birth, he would stay with our son because I couldn't bear the thought of him being whisked away without one of us at his side. We had discussed it for weeks leading up to today: Paul would follow our baby to the neighboring children's hospital, leaving me behind. He was hesitant at first as different scenarios played out in his mind—the "what-ifs." I wouldn't hear any of it. Our son would not be alone. If I couldn't be at his side, his daddy would be there, and they would have a piece of my broken heart with them.

He was our second child, our first son. His birth was quick, even quicker than the speedy delivery of our daughter. If we had another child, I would surely be the woman on the evening news whose baby wouldn't wait. Paul would be left with the task of delivering a third child on the side of the freeway. It's funny, considering his squeamish nature. The birth of our daughter nearly left him passed out on the delivery room floor. Yet, now, Paul sat upright and steadfast after dashing with our still-wet newborn to the emergency care he needed.

Our world had suddenly begun spinning with unbearable speed and intensity. With each passing moment my feelings of inadequacy and helplessness compounded, weighing heavily upon my chest. I was nearly breathless.

Paging Dr. Love

The administration of my epidural had been almost more than Paul could handle. Due to our circumstances, it was my only option. Pain meds would affect the baby, and he needed to be alert and drug-free. The suggestion of an epidural made me uneasy; the idea of placing what I imagined to be a three-inch needle in my spine was creepy. Who knew what might happen? A bit grudgingly, I decided to go ahead with it.

My labor nurse said that she would page Dr. Love and get us on the waiting list. *Dr. Love? Is that really what she said?* As she left the room, Paul and I looked at each other. Already both a bundle of nerves, we began to giggle and exchanged some rather juvenile jokes at poor Dr. Love's expense.

The nurse returned and said Dr. Love was on his second epidural and that we would be his third. Suddenly, Paul looked over at me, all comedy drained from his face, and demanded frantically, "Are you *sure* you want to do this? Are you sure it's safe? It's kind of freaking me out." He started regurgitating some of the rare complications of epidurals. "Can't women become paralyzed? I mean, if it's not done properly?" I had shared these tidbits with him during my first pregnancy. I guess he *had* been paying attention after all. "How am I going to take care of everything if you can't walk anymore? Seriously, are you going to let this guy named Dr. Love do this?"

I just stared back at him. He was on the edge of some sort of meltdown. We knew this was sure to be a very long day. Only God knew what was in store for us. But if this was how Paul was going to respond to something as simple as an epidural, what would happen when we made it to the big stuff? He was supposed to be composed, strong, and unwavering. Unbeknown to him, I had given him the assignment of being my *calm*. I was going to deliver this baby, and he was going to protect us. We wouldn't be afraid. In hindsight, maybe I should have let Paul in on my plan.

But things almost never go as expected, so at this point, I found myself comforting *him*. I told him women get epidurals every day and it was going to be just fine. I reminded him that it was my only option for pain relief, and that the nurse had explained that they do epidurals routinely in this hospital.

Nothing I said calmed him down. My frustration rose with each passing moment. My eyes narrowed as I slowly raised the outer corner of my heavy brow. I was finished with trying to talk him off a ledge. I resorted to my piercing stare and raised brow, an expression that Paul has lovingly coined "The Look." It conveyed my irritation: *I don't need you freaking out about every little thing today. I need you to be strong. I need to hear words of encouragement, not this stupidity about being paralyzed that you are giving to me now, because it's not helpful!*

Just then, Dr. Love came into the room and introduced himself. I looked at him, then to my husband, and then back to Dr. Love. I asked this fresh-faced young man in green scrubs, "You're Dr. Love? The anesthesiologist?" Yep, Dr.

Love looked to be about eighteen years old. I guess the joke was on us. I tried to persuade myself that he might be twenty. Now I wanted to take The Look back. *What if it's not done properly? Can't women become paralyzed from epidurals done by inexperienced twenty-year-old doctors with silly names? How will my husband take care of everything if I can't walk?*

I asked about the risks. We talked about the numbers. Dr. Love reassured me. He talked me down from my ledge, expressing that epidurals are routinely done at this hospital with a high success rate and almost no complications.

I decided to go ahead with it. I knew Paul wasn't happy, but he smiled through his fear, trying hard to put on a supportive face. As Dr. Love prepped me for the procedure, I teased him about his youthful appearance, referencing the '80s sitcom *Doogie Howser, M.D.* He made the point that youthfulness is a good quality, but also assured me that he was older than he looked. My husband sat on the windowsill, looking annoyed by this lighthearted banter. But for just a moment, the banter let me forget our special circumstances that had led us to this particular hospital, Abbott Northwestern, with its tunnel system connected to the highly respected Children's Hospital of Minnesota. I forgot, for just a sweet moment, until the nurse ran through my dry medical history, ending with "However, Baby does have a known heart defect."

The word "defect" dropped from her mouth and I heard its ugliness. The room suddenly felt cold and empty. I was annoyed with the perfectly lovely nurse whose words had jarred me back to reality. Awkward, painful silence filled the room now, until Dr. Love said quietly, "Okay, here we go."

I sat with my legs hanging over the side of the bed. Paul had moved to sit facing me. Surprisingly, the insertion of the needle was only mildly uncomfortable. It was followed by an odd, hollow "ping" noise that I wasn't sure was even audible within the room. I imagined a tiny little man nestled into the small of my back, a hat on his head and a teeny pitchfork in his hand. Strange, yes, but it isn't every day that a needle is placed into the small of your back.

Paul quickly said, "So is that it? Was it okay? Any complications?" Dr. Love reassured him that all had gone well. I could see the olive color return to my husband's face as thoughts of a wife crippled at the hands of a teenage doctor left his mind.

Once the room was empty and we had said our "thank-yous" to Dr. Love, Paul turned to me and said, "I can't believe you let him *do* that to you!"

"Do what to me?"

"Stick that needle in your back. I am so relieved that everything is okay, but what if something had happened? You were only his third patient!"

I began to giggle then, realizing why Paul had been so upset. "*Today*," I said firmly. "I was Dr. Doogie Howser's third patient this *morning*, not his third patient *ever!*"

Vines and Stars

I spent only an hour in labor. I lay on my side, the room darkened and my eyes shut. I pushed out the world and asked God for his presence. I was wearing a silver bracelet that had been a gift to me from a perfect stranger. It had an inscription on it from Matthew chapter 19, verse 26: "With God all things are possible." I had worn it each day since receiving it. It served as a constant reminder of God's presence. Lying there in labor, I clutched the bracelet tightly.

When my nurse came in to check on me, she was taken aback by the speed of my progress and said to Paul, "Well, Dad, are you ready to have this baby?" Then she rushed out of the room, announcing that she needed to make some phone calls. This was not a routine delivery, after all, and she needed all her ducks in a row—primarily, a team from Children's present and waiting.

As I was wheeled down a long hallway into an operating room, I lay on my back and watched the ceiling tiles shift and change. I spilled out my heart to God: *I know with You, all things are possible. Jesus, be with me. Jesus, make our baby's heart whole. Jesus, be with him. Jesus, provide healing. Heal him; heal us.*

The operating room was freezing. My mom was at my left and Paul at my right. Two nurses stood at my feet. One was the perfectly lovely nurse who had unwittingly jarred me back into reality during my epidural. She was a petite, middle-aged woman with a short, edgy pixie haircut. The other nurse had come in to help during delivery. I noticed her young face, fresh and pretty, and her arms, tattooed from collar bone to wrist with feminine designs of flowers, birds, and vines. The images were beautiful and vibrant. My doctor was there, too. She had requested hospital privileges at Abbott to be with me during delivery. She is smart and assertive, warm and compassionate, and I was thankful for her presence.

I lay in the quiet operating room, shivering. The air was heavy with pity and loss, with which I have become quite familiar since my baby's diagnosis. I'd grown tired, especially of the pity. It had impinged on my joy.

The team from Children's Hospital had arrived and was waiting in the adjacent room. It seemed I too was ready for delivery. Following a big contraction, I sat forward and pushed hard in response to my doctor's plea. An oxygen mask was placed upon my face, and I was told to breathe in deeply for my baby boy because his oxygen level was low and he was showing signs of distress. Panic started to fill the room. We waited for the next contraction, and I pushed hard again, as hard as I possibly could. My doctor reached down and grabbed onto the bedding underneath me, pulling it toward her and startling the nurses on either side. My pelvis was closer to her now, and my legs were super-extended in the stirrups. She was pulling so hard that I could see her arms shaking.

Then suddenly he was out and, just for a moment, placed on my belly as his umbilical cord was cut. It was quiet—no sound came from his lips—and then he was whisked away to the adjoining room, the hinged door swinging behind. I had only caught a glimpse of him. He looked like our beautiful daughter, except that his features were masculine. He had my husband's long torso and strong facial features.

A nurse came back for Paul. He stood wavering, not sure which room he belonged in. I pleaded with him to go with our son. I was left behind, lying in fear.

A window facing into the adjoining room allowed my doctor and nurses to see our baby. I studied their faces, looking for clues. They stood motionless. There was only silence. I started to realize how things must have looked beyond the operating room door. The pressure of it all began pushing me downward, to a place deep inside. I felt myself slipping into a distant, empty place where I'd never been before. It was icy and raw—my own quiet place for pain—and there I waited.

The neonatologist came into the operating room and explained how very sick our baby was. She said that they needed to take him away. She apologized and said that she rarely ever takes a child before Mom is able to hold him. But my son needed critical care, and they must go immediately. She would take Paul with her. I wanted to cry out. It wasn't supposed to happen this way! It was all too fast! I was supposed to hold him, even if just for a moment.

But I was forced to stay behind and wait until the effects of my epidural started to wear off. I tried not to think about it, but the thought kept creeping into my mind: *What if he dies and I never get a chance to hold him alive?* It seemed like an eternity before a new nurse was assigned to me and I was finally on my way to reunite with my baby. My nurse pushed me in a wheelchair, my mother walking at my side. We had no need to venture outside; instead, we navigated through the underground tunnel system. It must have been the way my son had come too.

We entered the basement of Children's and took the elevator to the second floor. The doors opened into a fresh space, new and bright. Cheerful children's artwork and multicolored stars adorned the hallways. Within this bright space were an Oncology floor, two Intensive Care Units, and operating rooms where open-heart surgery was performed on teeny chests.

We made our way through Security and into the Neonatal Intensive Care Unit, into the wing where my son lay. It was different than when we had toured just a few weeks ago. It was noisy and chaotic. About ten doctors and nurses huddled around one Isolette. I scanned the busy room to see Paul sitting on a tall stool in the corner, a nurse at his side. I looked at him and he motioned to where all the activity was. It was our little boy they were working on. His face was almost purple now. The image was crushing. I recoiled further into my icy, empty place.

His cardiologist, Dr. Singh, came over to greet me. He said they'd intubated him and confirmed with an ultrasound that, yes, indeed, he had Transposition of the Great Arteries. He explained the need to perform an emergency septostomy to create a hole in his heart allowing oxygen-rich blood to mix within the chambers. He said the pressure in his lungs was very high and he was getting little oxygen.

Dr. Singh then explained that he had just stepped away from the operating room where he'd been with another little one whose straightforward surgery had snowballed into a critical all-day event. He asked if his colleague, Dr. Gremmels, could perform the septostomy. Dr. Gremmels emerged from the heap of hands surrounding my son and explained that this was normally done in an operating room but that our son needed help *now*. They planned to perform the surgery right here in the NICU.

A nurse stepped in to lead Paul, my mom, and me away to wait elsewhere, but I desperately wanted to get a closer look at our baby before we left. I asked my nurse to push me near him, and as she did, one who was attending to him stepped aside, allowing me to see. He already had tubes and equipment coming from everywhere on his tiny body. Hands and voices swirled frantically around him. I could see him struggling, as if his whole body were gasping for air. Recognizing the urgency of his needs, I nodded to my nurse that I had seen enough. She backed my wheelchair away and the space closed in around him. My heart was painfully raw.

As we waited now in the Parent Sleep Room, I continuously asked for the time. I tried to calculate just how long he had been deprived of oxygen. My mind was clouded, leaving me unable to do simple math. I could have asked someone how long it had been, but I couldn't express myself either. I was paralyzed by my fear. *Lord, help us in this*, was the only thought that rang through my mind.

My mom gently asked Paul what had happened on their way here. He turned to me and asked if I wanted to know. "Of course I do," I said.

"They turned a corner, beyond where you could see, and that's when they started running with him, Mindy. I mean actually *running* with the Isolette through the tunnel system. We could hardly keep up. The doctor who came and told you she needed to take him, she had her arm interlocked in mine, and we tried to keep up, but we lagged behind. She told me how very sick he was and how they were trying to do everything they could to help him. She said that he hadn't responded well to their intervention. Then another team of doctors and nurses met us in the tunnel system. They had been running too. It was an unbelievable sight."

I was trying hard to process. *How could this be happening? I didn't even get to hold him. He was torn from me, and immediately had to fight to stay alive—how cruel.*

My epidural had almost completely worn off and pain started to penetrate my pelvis, but I kept it to myself. Finally, there was a knock at the door. Paul opened it to Dr. Gremmels, whose face showed no emotion. Dr. Singh squeezed into the tiny room behind him. I held my breath as Dr. Gremmels said, "The septostomy is finished, and your son's oxygen levels have significantly increased." He continued on, expressing how difficult the surgery had been. "It took several attempts to get the catheter through your son's septal wall."

"Thank you, thank you, for delivering at Abbott," Dr. Singh said. "He wouldn't have survived had you delivered him elsewhere." I exhaled, sensing we'd been led here by God's grace.

Fearfully, I asked, "What about the amount of time that he spent deprived of oxygen? Is it possible that there's brain damage?"

Dr. Singh quickly replied, "No. I'm not concerned." He explained that babies can manage with low oxygen levels for some time following birth. I sensed everyone's relief. I hadn't been the only one trying to do the math.

Our relief, however, would be short-lived. We would find out the following day that his brain had not gone unharmed.

Part II

A Tangled, Beautiful Mess

*W*e met a few months shy of my eighteenth birthday. It was crazy-intense, the kind of fire that keeps moms up at night. I noticed him long before we were introduced. He was hard to miss: There was the vintage VW Beetle and his *I'm not a Minnesota boy*, imported look. I caught his eye as well, reminding him of a girl he knew back home.

In my junior year of high school, I had met Paul's younger brother, John. We shared the same history class. John's English was sketchy at best. Our crotchety teacher would call on him and ask him to read aloud. The class listened in discomfort as he struggled. No one ever teased him. I didn't understand why the teacher singled him out like that, or why, on the other hand, he allowed him to blatantly cheat on tests and homework assignments. John would lean so far out of his own desk I was certain he would end up on the floor.

In the winter of my senior year, John started to date one of my friends. I was giddy when Jennifer called and said that she had met John's brother, Paul, and that all he wanted to talk about was me. Paul made her promise to call me the next day and ask if I would go out with him.

We met at Jennifer's parents' home. Paul came in through the entryway. He smiled at me, and in that first smile, I already knew. We hadn't even spoken, but I was completely taken with him. After that, we spent every available moment together. He was different than the rest of the boys I knew.

He was older, twenty when we met. He had wavy dark hair, strong features, and striking dark eyes. There was the accent too. I would have followed him to the end of the earth and jumped, had he jumped first.

He had a passion for art, Jim Morrison's The Doors, and everything Volkswagen. He was kind and considerate, and he worked hard at trying to impress my family. He never seemed to notice how small the two-bedroom apartment I shared with my mother and stepfather was.

Paul had come to the States three years earlier at the age of seventeen. His parents made certain that each of their three sons left Syria prior to turning eighteen, thus avoiding Syria's mandatory military service commitment. They had enjoyed a comfortable lifestyle in the Middle East, yet they desired more for their family—more opportunity, more freedom.

Paul's parents' expectations were high for all their boys. Paul didn't speak a word of English when he arrived. He spent hours each day studying the dictionary. Much to his English teacher's delight, he started speaking the language only weeks after his arrival. In a mere six months, he was fluent. Her delight contrasted with his father's disappointment. To a man who had easily mastered five languages, six months was an eternity.

There was an enormous amount of pressure for Paul to succeed academically. He had attended a private, rigid Armenian Catholic school in Syria, where he struggled in the heavily structured classrooms. It's easy to recognize how bright he is. In fact, he's the smartest person I've ever known. He is a wealth of knowledge, especially in history and political science. He has the most incredible memory. Yet, school suffocated him. He hated almost every moment, both in Syria and in the U.S.

His family's expectations were quite different from those of my family. Of course mine wanted me to do well. But their definition of "doing well" was different from Paul's parents'. They were happy that I was finishing high school, and even happier that I wanted to attend college. They were respectful of the choices I made. Their expectations were simply that I would work hard, whatever path I chose.

My family opened both their door and their hearts to Paul. They enjoyed his company, expressing interest in who he was. They found him funny and smart. Paul always greeted my mom with a kiss on the cheek. She ate it up, enamored of his ridiculous charm. If you were in Paul's presence, chances are you were smiling.

Paul's family didn't have the same regard for me. They were icy at first. They had notions about American girls. Truth be told, I was a poster girl for all that can go wrong in the American family. My parents had divorced when I was only five years old. My father lived 1500 miles away with his fourth wife and one of my half-brothers. My mother had remarried for the third time. I had two older half-sisters, neither one married and each with a son. As if that didn't seem bad enough to Paul's parents, hold on to your hats, people . . . we didn't have a church. In fact, we had *never* had a church. That's right—I came from a divorce-stricken, god-less, American family. In the big picture of how to get your boyfriend's Middle Eastern Catholic family to like and accept you, well . . . let's just say I had my work cut out for me.

People are people. My upbringing and Paul's were, literally, a world apart from each other. Yet, when you strip some of the junk away, we were more alike than we were ever different. My family was a train wreck of broken marriages and half-siblings scattered all over the country, yet I never felt broken or alone. I was supported and loved as a child, regardless of my circumstances. Paul's family pushed him hard to succeed. Still, he understood that they loved him and wanted the very best for him.

We were married in the fall of 1996. I was just twenty-one years old. Once it was clear that I wasn't just a phase Paul was going through, my in-laws grew to love me. I loved them too. Sticky cultural differences arose from time to time, but for the most part, we worked through them. We developed an appreciation for one another. Imagine the 2002 romantic comedy *My Big Fat Greek Wedding*. Paul's family mirrored the family of the lovable Greek-American main character, Toula, so closely that we practically had to pick ourselves up off the movie theater's sticky floor. Paul, like Toula, even had a passionate non-English-speaking grandparent who wandered the house cursing the Turks for their inhumanity. The differences were, I wasn't raised in a straitlaced household like Ian Miller, Toula's love interest, was, and Paul and my family had had an instant fondness for each other.

We bought a tiny house in St. Paul, Minnesota. We were happy. Paul worked hard, and I juggled both work and school.

We were married five years when our baby girl came into the world and turned life as we knew it upside down. We chose the name Sophia because we thought it was beautiful. *She* was beautiful. Mothering a newborn is impossible to prepare for. My own needs instantly became secondary. The sleep deprivation alone was horrifying—no wonder it's used as a torture method. Then there's the part where you go without bathing every day, like you're camping on the North Shore of Lake Superior. Meals were mediocre at best, and almost always cold. All of this with the overwhelming sense of responsibility that came with knowing she would call me "Mommy."

Nor could I have prepared for the incredible amount of joy that filled every fragment of my exhausted body. I was captivated by her. I would never be the same. What a tangled, beautiful mess.

Skeleton Keys

*O*ur home in the city was impossibly tiny after the arrival of our sweet Sophie. This little person required so much stuff. We were so proud of our house on Gorman Avenue—all 749 square feet of it. Though it had been built during World War II, we were only the tiny rambler's second owners. The original occupants had lived there for nearly sixty years. They never had children. Sophie was the first baby to lay her head down there.

Our real estate agent described our house as "adorable and cute" in our "For Sale" ad. The house had one itty-bitty bathroom. We had two small bedrooms, with 1940s (which is to say *small*) closets. While seated in the "eat-in" kitchen, Paul was able to reach for things inside a cabinet without getting up. The doors had old skeleton-key holes, and the knobs were made of ornate glass. Somehow the woodwork had escaped a paint brush all those years. The doors and crown molding were still beautiful, done in a rich cherry finish. All charm aside, "adorable and cute" also meant terribly small.

Sophie was a year and a half old when we put our tiny home on the market. It sold five days later. We had found a bigger, newer home, and we were so excited. Even so, one afternoon as moving day quickly approached, I called Paul at work. I was a sobbing mess. I had been packing, and our house's charm had worked its way inside me—seller's regret, I guess. What if the new owners didn't love it the way we had? How would they appreciate all the sweat we had poured into it to get it to this clean, fresh state? Besides, it was our *home*. We had proudly hung our wedding pictures here, fresh from the photographer. We brought Sophie here straight from the hospital, whispering in her ear that she was home. It housed all our "firsts." How could we leave it behind?

He let me cry it out like any reasonable husband would. He promised new memories in a new house that was sure to become a home, and with that, we loaded the baby gear, the wedding pictures, and all the rest into a moving truck.

Toddler Giggles and Cut Screen Doors

*O*ur new home was a four-bedroom fifteen-year-old split-level in a modest suburban neighborhood. We thought we might never find furniture to fill up this new space. The yard was big, and we were thrilled to see Sophie have a place to run and play.

We'd been in our new home only a couple of days. I was off to work that busy morning. Paul's plan for the day was to tie up some loose ends from the weekend move and continue unpacking. After a morning of errands that took Paul and Sophie across town and back again, they returned to the new house to find it stuffy and unbearable. It was mid-August, after all, and we hadn't yet tried out the house's air conditioning.

Coming home to a stuffy house may not seem like a big deal to most people, but Paul isn't most people. He doesn't "do" heat or humidity. You would think a little heat would call to his mind some fond childhood memories: summers spent on the coast of Lebanon, hours playing on the beach with his brothers, swimming in the Mediterranean Sea, the thick, humid air filling his lungs. Not so much. Not in our house, not with the modern advances of AC at his fingertips. Hot summer nights in our house are spent with me in long-sleeved PJs, trying to make a warm little space for myself under the covers, while Paul lies next to me, on top of the covers, wearing only his boxer briefs and a smile. He is happy, and cooler than a cucumber.

So, on this particular hot day, Paul and Sophie came through the front door. Immediately, he started dropping his clothes onto the floor, leaving only his briefs on as he walked through to open the sliding-glass door leading onto the deck. He closed and locked the screen door to keep little Miss Sophie inside. He thought he'd air out the house for just a moment or two and then turn on the AC.

In the meantime, Paul decided to work on getting our computer hooked up and ventured out into the attached garage where the computer had been left during the move. Had he been wearing a coat, Sophie would have been right on his coattails. He told her to wait in the hallway, not wanting her to follow him into the garage that was even hotter than the house. "Daddy will be right back," he said as the door to the garage closed behind him. He walked over to the boxes labeled "office" and picked one up. As he turned back to the door, holding the computer box, he heard the lock on the inside door knob turn and click. It took a minute to register: *Oh no, my toddler has just locked me inside my garage!* Rushing to the door, he tried to turn the knob. Yep, it was locked, all right. So, trying to remain calm, he started with a gentle request: "Sophie, honey? Sophie? Are you there?"

A little voice said, "Dada? Dada!"

"Sophie, honey, I need you to open the door for me. Can you let Dada back inside?" But there was no sound. Paul tried again: "Sophie, you need to turn the knob so I can get back inside." A giggle, then more giggles—sweet little giggles were all he heard . . . then the sound of pint-sized sandaled feet trotting down the hallway and away from the garage door.

Paul took another minute to digest his predicament. *Okay,* he thought, *so, I'm locked out of the house and my daughter is locked inside the house. I haven't yet met my neighbors, and I am not wearing any clothes.* Yes, the absence of clothes definitely complicated things. How could he possibly introduce himself, explain his predicament, and ask for help while standing at someone's front door in his undies? Weighing his options, Paul thought about his eighteen-month-old "exploring" the new house, completely unattended. There were half-open boxes of all sorts of things scattered all over, not to mention that she hadn't yet mastered the art of climbing stairs. Somehow, he needed to break into his new home from the outside—in his underwear. He remembered he had opened the back sliding-glass door. His only obstacle would be the locked screen door. Looking through the garage, he found a box cutter, the kind with a razor that pushes out from one end. He pushed the button to open the garage door, hoping and praying he wouldn't see anyone outside. Full sun streamed into the garage, a spotlight illuminating his every naked move. *Oh, dear God,* he prayed, *please don't let anyone see me.* Peeking out of the garage and seeing no one, he headed for the back yard. Alas, the back side of the property lined a busy street; traffic hummed by.

Reaching the deck, Paul could see Sophie through the sliding door. She waved to him, saying, "Hi, Dada, hi!" He tried to get her to unlock the screen door, but she just thought this was a fun game they were playing and ran away. He hesitated for a moment. This door was part of a thirty-year mortgage he'd signed a mere forty-eight hours ago. Then he took another look at himself standing in his undies on his deck, box cutter in hand, cars passing by in the distance. He decided that some things you just need to chalk up to a good story. He cut a hole in the screen door big enough to slide his hand through, and unlocked the door. Sophie was safe and giggly as ever inside.

A new memory had been made in our new house.

Unchurched

*I*n the fall of 1999, Paul and I joined a couples group at our church. Hosanna!, a big vibrant church, encourages parishioners to join a small group with people of similar life-stages or interests. My faith was new. The idea of connecting with people of faith was both intriguing and overwhelming to me. We were matched with five other couples, all of us newly married and in our twenties.

We met one night a week, first at the church, then in each other's homes. We studied the Bible. We laughed. We prayed for one another. Despite the similarities that brought us together as a group, we were very different from each other. We would not have formed these friendships organically. Our faith united us, and through it, we developed intimate friendships. We supported each other through a number of life challenges: career changes, family problems, financial difficulties, mental illness, pregnancies, surgeries, relocations, and the death of a parent. Life got messy. The list was long and sticky.

The fact that I found myself in this place, surrounded by believers who openly prayed for one another, was the culmination of a separate journey of sorts.

I had spent my teens and early twenties dancing with the concept of faith. I couldn't deny my attraction to it. Being part of the "un-churched" left me feeling spiritually inadequate. My mother's experience with the Catholic Church had been thorny at best. Thus, her distance from such things, and, in turn, mine.

My mother went to a Catholic grade school. Students attended Mass every morning, and my mother would often pass out during Mass. She said the air was thin, and for some reason she had a difficult time breathing. One of the nuns, who didn't care much for my mother, decided she was faking. She treated her fainting episodes as a behavioral problem. Each time my mother passed out, the nun would strike her.

In the fall of 1966, my mother was a pregnant, scared teenage girl. When my grandmother found out about the pregnancy, my mother was forced into marriage. Her young husband joined the army, and when my oldest sister, Dawn, was just six weeks old, they left for an army base in Germany. Feeling guilty over her quick courthouse wedding, my mother sought out an army chaplain and asked him to bless her marriage. He refused. The chaplain said he couldn't imagine doing so—not for a marriage such as hers. Two years later, my sister Tammy was born. A handful of years later, they divorced. It was then, after her divorce, that she was told she had been excommunicated from the church. She never returned.

The gentle tug of faith on my heart had always been there. From the time I was just a young girl, I knew there was this hollow piece of me tucked somewhere deep inside. When I was sixteen years old, I sought out a pastor and asked for baptism. It was my first effort to respond to the tugging at my heart. My mother supported me in my decision.

However, after my baptism, I didn't return to the church. Still, the pull at my heart remained.

This group of faithful peers, and this vibrant, welcoming church helped me respond to the stirring of my heart. It was just the "church" I needed.

Friends in a Buick

Paul and I felt especially connected to one couple in particular, Doug and Brooke.

Relating to one another was easy. It was the friendship that every couple looks for. Both you and your spouse enjoy their company. You can discuss anything with them. There was nothing uncomfortable to work through. There wasn't that thing that your husband can't stand about her. He doesn't drive you nuts either. There wasn't any pompous *yuck* that undermines a friendship. "Hey, I got this promotion, car, house, etc . . . well, aren't I great . . ." All of that was missing from this relationship. There was only laughter and warmth. Years will pass, and we'll be that foursome you see getting into a Buick and leaving a Bakers Square, the men in the front seat, the blue-haired ladies in the back. We'll be friends for decades, becoming family to each other.

Doug and Brooke were married the spring before the four of us met. They'd been friends since childhood. At just fourteen, Brooke told her mom that someday she would marry Doug. Doug remembers chasing her around, trying to kiss her at birthday parties and such. He is warm and caring, just like Paul. Brooke is innately thoughtful and generous. She's a friend who would get up in the middle of the night and drive across town without a second thought if you needed help.

They had their first child, a daughter, a year before Sophie was born. Elizabeth's delivery came with complications. Brooke needed uterine surgery immediately following. A few weeks later, on Easter Sunday, they found themselves back at the hospital. Brooke was hemorrhaging again, and another operation took place.

As if adjusting to parenthood and Brooke's unexpected health problems hadn't been stressful enough for their family, Elizabeth was diagnosed with a cataract and glaucoma. They were crushed. Their sweet baby girl would need eye surgery.

In an attempt to put her surgery into the realm of the big picture, Brooke's doctor pointed out that in that same building, some babies had open-heart surgery. They had no idea at the time, but through the doctor's words, God was whispering to them of things to come.

Less than two years later, Doug and Brooke had their second child, a baby boy they named Blake. During a routine ultrasound, Brooke had learned about Blake's "special heart." Her technician had seemed fixated on the image of the baby's heart, prompting Brooke to mention that she had a brother who had died in infancy of a heart defect. Doug and Brooke soon found themselves in a perinatology office, with a congenital heart defect diagnosis. Their life was turned upside down.

Brooke's perinatologist had a German name—Dr. Franken-something or other—but, because she was a very unkind woman, Brooke referred to her as "Dr. Frankenstein." Dr. Frankenstein openly blamed Brooke for her son's heart defect, stating that Brooke's "uncontrolled" gestational diabetes had caused it. Brooke carried tremendous guilt over this for months, until a conversation with Blake's cardiologist softened it. He was appalled at Dr. Frankenstein's comments, expressing to Brooke that nothing she had done had caused Blake's defect. Her diabetes was managed to the best of her ability. At any rate, he did not believe gestational diabetes was to blame at all.

Blake was born prematurely. His heart defect was complex, with both a narrowing of his aorta, known as coarctation, and valve deficiencies. He, like Charlie two and a half years later, was born at Abbott. He too had a host of doctors and nurses waiting for his arrival. He too needed resuscitation following his birth. He too was rushed through the tunnel system, his distraught father lagging behind. He too needed emergency surgery in order to survive.

Paul and I witnessed Doug and Brooke's strength during all of this. I couldn't imagine the pain they were in. But Brooke approached each new challenge—and there were plenty—with extreme optimism. She always had a smile on her face. Her response, during the pregnancy and afterward, was often "He is going to be okay; maybe not right away, but in the end, he is going to be okay." Honestly, half our conversations during that time ended with me questioning her sanity. I wondered where her fear was. But she expressed that she felt God had his hand on Blake.

After Blake recovered from his first heart surgery—a septostomy, just like Charlie's—they sent him home, tiny and frail. He needed to be bigger and stronger before going back for another surgery.

I was uncomfortable around him. He was approaching six months but didn't even weigh ten pounds. His coloring was dreadful, like that of an elderly man inching his way toward death. His lips were bluish, and he had dark circles around his eyes. His arms and legs were extremely thin and gangly. He hadn't made the milestones that parents look for: rolling over, sitting up, attempts at crawling.

At the same time, I sensed something very special in Blake's presence. His smile lit up the whole room, as if to say, "God has his hand on me, I am happy, and I am cared for." He was handsome, poor color and all. His hair was thick and wavy in a "cupid" kind of way. His brown eyes had an unusual depth to them, as if he already had a story to tell. His parents—well, his parents were exhausted.

Blake would have two more heart surgeries, as well as a surgery to correct a malrotation of the bowel. Doug and Brooke entered each new challenge optimistically. They were brave. How were they managing these obstacles? I couldn't begin to picture myself in their position. I couldn't even keep from crying during Sophie's well-child visits with her pediatrician, as her tears from a needle poke brought tears to my eyes. I wondered how parents have the strength to hand their baby over to a surgeon. . . .

Sweeping Awareness

*I*t was early in my second pregnancy, and I sat alone in reflection. Worship was full that brisk fall Sunday morning. Sophie's arrival had transformed the life we once knew. I
considered all the ways in which our life might change again
as we welcomed a new baby. My reflection was full of joy-
ful anticipation, and then, in an instant, something changed.
Like a wave, it swept through my core. It was inaudible, and
yet it resonated within every part of me. It settled deep within my heart. It was intense awareness: Something was wrong
with my baby.

Surely every pregnant woman worries some about her
baby's health, but this was different. I told Paul there was
something wrong with the baby, that I was sure of it. Like
any good husband, he kept telling me that everything was
fine. He reminded me that I worried when I was pregnant
with Sophie too, and he was right, I had. But this time it was
different. This worry was woven into my core.

There wasn't any medical reason for my concern. We
had conceived easily with both pregnancies. We had had a
healthy baby girl just two years earlier. There were no complications this time either. I was young and healthy.

As we approached my twentieth week of pregnancy, my
OB-GYN decided to send me for a Level II ultrasound. She
noticed that my placenta was positioned low and anteriorly.

It wasn't overly concerning, but nonetheless, having a Level II ultrasound made sense.

Our ultrasound was scheduled at a perinatology office. We brought our Sophie, thinking it would be fun for her to see her little brother or sister. Having her along distracted me from the unease I had woken with that morning. With our cute button-nosed, piggy-tailed toddler in tow, we walked into the clinic. La-Z-Boy loungers were lined up against the wall of the waiting area. A sign on the wall said "Reserved for Patients on Bed Rest." Of course, seeing this sign only intrigued my husband. He looked around and, seeing no other pregnant women waiting, just *had* to try one out, even if just for a moment or two. It was all about the sign, really.

We chatted with Sophie, asking if she would prefer a baby sister or a baby brother. Today, like most times, it was a sister, but occasionally she would say a brother. Most of the time she simply humored us in her curiously mature way.

Finally, we were called back into an ultrasound room. I hoisted myself up onto the bed. The goop was squirted onto my belly, and the technician started her images and measurements. She asked us if we wanted to know the sex of the baby. We expressed that, yes, we would like very much to know.

The technician's name was Amy; she was young and sweet. Her face was fresh, and she wore her hair pulled back in a low ponytail. She looked about six months pregnant herself. I asked her if she knew what she was having, and she smiled and said yes. "It's a girl," she said. "How could I not know?" She expressed that the anticipation, coupled with the on-the-job opportunity to find out at any time, would have made it impossible to wait.

I told her how we had been opposed to finding out the sex of a child before the baby's birth. Babies are a gift from God. It wouldn't be right to open early. She smiled, and I said, "Well, that was until I got pregnant, and then, well, we opened early! . . . I would like to open early today too, you know, for just a little peek."

"Well, this is a little boy," she said, smiling.

I looked over at Paul. His face was filled with surprise and joy. "Really, a boy?" he said.

That was my response too. "Really? A boy?" I questioned. I was the youngest of three girls; I had a little girl. Girls I can do; girls are what I know. But what would I do with a little boy?

Paul smiled down at Miss Sophie, who by this point had become rather restless. She was jumping onto and off of the step stool at the side of the bed.

Amy said, "Sophie, you're going to have a little brother!" Sophie simply paused for a moment and said nonchalantly, "Okay," then continued hopping on and off the stool. Not exactly the response we had hoped for.

As Amy took a few more pictures, her demeanor changed; she seemed more focused. She kept returning to the same images—the baby's heart. Paul and I looked at each other in fear. Amy asked if we had gotten the "triple test" done. The triple test screened for chromosomal disorders. I quickly told her we had decided against the test.

Paul finally asked, "Is there something wrong?" Amy never answered him. Instead, she said we would see one of the doctors as soon as she was finished. She left the room a couple of times, images in hand, only to return a few minutes later to get more.

Finally, we met the perinatologist, a stocky, good-looking, middle-aged man. He had kind eyes and spoke tenderly. He said he had concerns with the images of our baby's heart. He looked again for what seemed like the hundredth time. My back ached. My heart ached. Sophie had long since lost her patience, and Paul's patience was razor thin as well.

The doctor finally looked up from the ultrasound machine. He seemed reluctant, as if knowing that what he had to say would be difficult. "Your baby has a heart defect," he said softly. He explained that he thought he saw a hole in our baby's heart and that he suspected that the baby might also have a complex structural heart defect. As Amy had done, he asked if we had had the triple test done, explaining that there was sometimes a correlation between chromosomal defects and heart defects. He said we would need to see a pediatric cardiologist in order to get a more definitive diagnosis.

Fear, but not disbelief, came over me. After all, I had known that something was wrong; this was just an affirmation for me. Paul had more to digest. Sweet little Sophie—I envied her in this moment. Her life was just as it had been this morning.

We left the office with possible diagnoses scribbled across a piece of paper, along with an appointment made with a pediatric cardiologist the following week.

My first phone call as soon as we got back in the car was to Brooke, and it was the easiest one to make. After all, Brooke understood what it was like to learn your baby had a heart defect. She understood *me*, in this moment, better than anyone else.

"Brooke, it's a boy . . . and there is something wrong with his heart."

Brooke had anticipated a call from us, but was unprepared to hear these details. She tried to offer support through her own blinding disbelief. She asked about possible diagnoses and told me that things were going to be okay. She said that *we* were going to be okay.

The more phone calls we made—the more we told the news—the more it sank in. I just wanted to retreat home and hide away. But at home, this uninvited truth boldly followed us right through the front door.

I sat on the couch in our living room. My head pounded. My breathing became labored. The room started to spin, slowly at first. Then gradually the momentum of the room turning around me increased. Or was it me spinning, within the room? I lay down, trying to calm myself. The movement came from deep within my core. I had lost control. I had lost control of my circumstances, and now it seemed I was losing control of my body. It was all spinning away from me—my plans, what my life was supposed to look like. It was spiraling into a distant place, as if a storm had come and ripped it from my arms. Maybe I hadn't held onto it tightly enough. Maybe God didn't understand my limitations. I was full of fear. *What is going to happen to us? How can I face this?*

When the spinning finally stopped, my body became warm and flushed, as if a heated blanket had been wrapped around me. The top of my head started to tingle. The feeling intensified and swirled downward, wrapping, embracing my body. With this physical calm came a new awareness. I knew with absolute certainty that my son had no chromosomal deficiencies. I never worried about it again. Later, I would decline the amniocentesis; what would be the point? I also knew with certainty that he was going to be okay . . . eventually.

I spent that weekend alone at home. Paul worked, and Sophie spent time with her grandma. I tossed and turned in the nights. Each time I woke, I tried to convince myself that this had just been one of those wild pregnancy dreams. I got out of bed and went across the hall to the mostly empty nursery. The walls were white and bare. We had wanted to know whether we were having a boy or a girl before we started decorating. That seemed silly now.

I moved the glider chair in front of the large bedroom window. The midnight sky was dreary. I rocked back and forth, as if to comfort a newborn baby. Only, it was my own pain I was trying to ease. With tears streaming down my face and falling onto my round belly, my pajamas growing increasingly wet, I cradled my son. I held him safe within. I cried out, releasing the tension and pain from my body. At first, there were no words—just cries and moans of grief. Grief—I mourned the child I thought I was supposed to have. It was the death of my *healthy* baby boy.

Then the requests came. I cried out to Jesus to save my son. I asked repeatedly for him to be healed, for him to be saved. I asked Jesus to be with me, to help me. I asked for strength. I asked and I asked until I had exhausted myself, and until I was certain he heard me.

Knit Together

*W*e were given a few days between that first diagnosis—"something is wrong with your baby's heart; we just aren't sure what"—and a follow-up ultrasound with a pediatric cardiologist. Supposedly, the cardiologist would give us a better idea of what was going on. It had been a few days now since I spent that first weekend crying alone in the baby's nursery. I was wrapping my mind around how things might look for us now.

The night before our follow-up ultrasound, we met with our small group for prayer. We had called on them, and without hesitation, they were there, gathering with us at the church where we had all first met.

The church's prayer chapel is inviting and pleasant, candlelit and quiet. Comfy loveseats are positioned around the room, creating intimate seating areas. The chapel is staffed with volunteers, one of whom met us as Brooke led us in. I noticed a few other people quietly praying. The prayer volunteer, Susan, asked what kind of prayer needs we had, and Brooke told her that we had come to pray for healing. Simply stated, that was our intention.

Susan smiled brightly and said, "Well, then, that is just what we'll do, and we will do so boldly."

I was a bit put off by her eager response. Susan would later express to me how she had been drawn into the prayer chapel only moments before our arrival. She hadn't been

44

on the prayer team volunteer schedule that evening, but she had felt called into the chapel with thoughts of healing on her heart. Our immediate arrival must have been a striking "God moment" for her. Over time, and as I got to know her better, I became more comfortable with Susan's way of approaching God. Why *shouldn't* we be bold in our requests?

Brooke filled Susan in on our group's history, and how we had been here for prayer when Brooke had found herself in this very same situation two years ago: she, too, pregnant with a baby boy; she, too, told he had a heart problem; she, too, surrounded by this same group of friends. Brooke expressed that being here again, praying for the very same thing, felt both remarkable and frightening. The parallels in our lives seemed a bit much to be chalked up to coincidence, and in that, there was both comfort and fear for us both.

Susan was impressed by the supportive nature of our small group, commenting on how nice it was that they had all come to support Paul and me. She had me sit on a chair in the middle of the room. Paul stood behind me with his hands on my shoulders, and everyone else circled around and reached out to touch either Paul or me. I lay my hands on my belly. Susan anointed my belly with warm, soothing oil, making the sign of the cross with her finger.

Roxanne, my best friend since forever and ever, was there, kneeling at my left side. I was grateful for her presence; she had known and loved me before all of this. Melissa was there, kneeling at my right side. Melissa and her husband Jeff were the latest addition to our group; they had started meeting with us about two years prior. Susan's husband Larry came in just before we started to pray, and Susan filled him in on the extraordinary circumstances that had led us here.

As the praying started, my nervousness quickly faded. Susan quoted Scripture, mostly Psalm 139:

> *I could ask the darkness to hide me*
> *and the light around me to become night—*
> *but even in darkness I cannot hide from you.*
> *To you the night shines as bright as day.*
> *Darkness and light are the same to you.*
>
> *You made all the delicate, inner parts of my body*
> *and knit me together in my mother's womb.*
> *Thank you for making me so wonderfully complex!*
> *Your workmanship is marvelous—how well I know it.*
> *You watched me as I was being formed in utter seclusion,*
> *as I was woven together in the dark of the womb.*
> *You saw me before I was born.*
> *(Psalm 139:11-16, New Living Translation)*

Susan focused on verses 13, 14, and 15, expressing how God was knitting my son together in my womb, how God saw him even in seclusion and knew every piece of his little heart. She asked that God would make his heart whole, expressing at the same time that we respected his workmanship.

Larry addressed the potential chromosomal deficiency, asking God to touch him in that way, so that he might be free of such a problem.

Larry and Susan addressed the fear within our group and asked Jesus to take it from us, and to wrap us instead in comfort. Their prayer was that we would continue to be a blessing to one another. It was powerful and brought us to tears.

One by one, our friends made their requests: that Jesus would touch us, that we would find comfort, that he would give us strength. Mostly, they simply prayed for our baby's heart, that it would be made whole. Brooke's prayer was intimate, as she knew this place I was in better than anyone.

I felt drawn to Melissa as she prayed for us. We hadn't known each other long, and I didn't know her as intimately as I did the others. Yet, in that moment, it was her voice I heard, with all the others falling away. Her requests for my baby were organic and pure. None of us could ever have imagined at the time a third baby boy born among us with a broken heart—that notion would have seemed wildly absurd—but Melissa would have her time too.

The room was candlelit, but as the prayers continued, light came from somewhere within me—or near me—I'm not sure which. It flooded over my eyelids. With it came comfort and warmth, as if I'd stumbled into a warm spring day.

Others, strangers, joined us in our requests, working their way closer to our circle. They started to form a second circle surrounding Paul and me. A petite older woman came into the circle. I presumed she was another volunteer. I don't know her name, and I regret now that I never took time to study her face. Her focus was our fear. She asked for

God's peace and comfort for us. She expressed her certainty of God's presence; she spoke of light she had seen rain down on us as she had watched from across the room. Her voice was sweet. I felt the tension that encircled us dissolve, and in its place came a host of emotions. I heard weeping all around me.

We had been there two years before, praying for Blake's heart. We didn't know what his adversity would look like. But now we knew.

Blake was a blessing. He embodied the gift of life. He taught us perseverance. However, there was another side. We had watched him suffer. We had watched Doug and Brooke suffer too. Two years in, and the journey already seemed long. Now, here we were, Paul and I, starting our own journey. We knew our journey would be our own. Nonetheless, knowing Doug and Brooke, we had a sense of what the road looked like.

I grasped onto my faith, because I was broken on my own.

Cork Boards

I fell in and out of sleep that evening. The time spent awake wasn't restless; rather, it was thoughtful. I made all my requests known to God. I left nothing unsaid, and I knew he was listening. God was there. I was held, enclosed in his arms, and that made all the difference.

Our drive to the clinic that morning wasn't without worry or concern. Nevertheless, an amount of disappointment was now tucked away behind me. I felt peace with whatever the outcome might be. Pieces of me were filled with optimism. Maybe we had been given miraculous healing; we had asked boldly for it. Maybe this was over, and it would turn into a pregnancy story to share with girlfriends over coffee and scones. Maybe my regular life would return. Maybe it would look like the morning we headed out the door with our pigtailed toddler to find out if she was going to have a sister or a brother. Or . . . maybe what had seemed like a bizarre pregnancy dream just days ago would be my new reality. After all, there had been that *knowing* since early in my pregnancy that I was never able to put to rest. Either way, what I knew without hesitation was that I was held.

We checked in with the receptionist at the Pediatric Heart Clinic. The waiting room was empty; there wasn't a child in sight. I was disappointed. I wanted so badly to see a child, one whose heart was or had been broken. I wanted to see what they looked like. I wanted to watch them in action, to see them run and play like children do. Was that silly? But I couldn't help it, and it made me feel childlike and ignorant.

I fidgeted with the row of pamphlets laid out on a table. I picked up one that said "Camp Odayin" on the cover. It's a summer camp for kids with heart defects. The camp "puts worries to rest" as it is staffed with pediatric cardiologists and cardiac nurses. Campers explore the outdoors through athletic and creative activities, all in a "safe and medically supervised environment." Kids build long-lasting friendships with other kids who have similar emotional, medical, and social concerns, the pamphlet said.

I was sure that I didn't want my child to go there. I'd want to send him off to a camp someday, but not this one. I'd want to send him to a YMCA camp and worry about him climbing trees. I'd want to worry about ticks and bug bites. I was sure Camp Odayin was great for these kids with broken hearts, but I just wanted the YMCA.

We were called back for our consultation. I returned the pamphlet to its place, hoping to never see it again. We were led down a hallway lined with cork boards packed with photographs of children, all holiday-dressed and smiling. It was hard not to notice all the cherub faces with Down syndrome.

We entered the exam room, and I hoisted myself up onto the table. Our sonographer this morning was a middle-aged man. We exchanged pleasantries, and I settled in. I exposed my belly and he slopped on the goop. He started at square one, of course, as they all do. He seemed to take a hundred measurements around every little thing. Every little thing, that is, but our son's heart.

The receptionist poked her head in the door to let us know that our doctor had been held up at the hospital. Finally, the tech started taking images of the baby's heart. He did it methodically; I studied his face for the slightest clue that something might be wrong, but he seemed unimpressed with the images before him. A phone rang in the exam room. He picked it up and I could hear the doctor's voice on the other end. She was on her way to the clinic, and asked about our ultrasound. He said, "No, not that I can see . . . No, no, I don't think so . . . Okay then, we'll see you in a bit." Paul and I shot a look to each other to say, *Holy cow, really? Can he really not see anything?* Paul was already grinning. He's quicker than I to go to a place where things are okay.

When the doctor arrived a few minutes later, she knocked lightly and came in. She introduced herself, giving an impressively long name that didn't stick with me. She was young and of Indian descent. She had shoulder-length jet-black hair and dark, pretty eyes. She spent the next few minutes looking over the images, as I held my breath.

She requested another image, so the technician asked me to change positions and came back with his wand and goop.

As they worked, they chatted about a baby born that morning. Their voices were hushed, but they failed to appreciate how Paul and I studied their every move. I felt as though we'd walked into a private conversation. It made me uncomfortable, but I was not in a position to excuse myself. Part of me wanted to hear. I wanted a glimpse into her world. They whispered about how tiny the baby was, how low her oxygen level was, and how blue she had been when she arrived. Her defect had gone undetected before birth, and it took them too long to have her transported. She didn't know how they'd approach a surgical fix, and she was uncertain of the outcome. I thought about the baby's mother and the pain she must be in.

Paul brought their attention back to us by asking whether they were able to get the image they wanted. She looked at both of us and said, "Well, I've seen enough to tell you that this is a healthy baby with a healthy heart." Paul and I looked at each other. Relief and joy covered his face, while I returned a cautious smile. I wanted so badly to believe her, but still I was hesitant. I asked her whether she saw anything concerning—anything at all. She said she couldn't rule out a small hole in the heart, because sometimes it's difficult to detect them on ultrasound. But she assured us that a small hole rarely requires surgery, and that they often close on their own.

I couldn't leave it alone, and I questioned her again as to whether she had seen all that she needed to. I mentioned once more that the perinatologist suspected a complex defect. She smiled and said, "I don't see anything that would suggest that." She humored me by saying that she would be happy to take a look again, after our son was born.

Feeling unsettled and foggy, I relied on Paul to lead me out of the office. As we stood waiting for the elevator,

Paul kissed me and said, "It's over. Didn't you hear what she said—healthy baby, healthy heart?"

I stood at a crossroads. Was I to embrace and accept this? Had we really received miraculous healing: "You were once disease-stricken, but now you've been healed"? I'd never doubted the existence of miraculous healing. But . . . could it really have happened to *me*? I was certain that something amazing had happened the night before, but *this*? Paul and I discussed how the images from our first ultrasound looked different than the ones we had seen today. But I wasn't about to pretend to know what I was looking at, and neither was he. So I said it out loud again, to Paul.

"She said, 'Healthy baby, healthy heart,' right?" I knew what I had heard, but I needed him to say it again.

"Yes, 'healthy baby, healthy heart.' That's what the woman said. She's a specialist, Mindy. I think she knows what she's talking about."

I chose to believe that things were going to be okay. When the doubts crept in, I did my best to push them away. When people asked about our son and his heart, I shared. I told them that I had had a powerful experience in a prayer chapel the night before a follow-up ultrasound, and the following day the cardiologist couldn't find anything wrong. These were my truths, and while I often felt apprehension in sharing, I did so anyway.

I shared the details of my experience in the prayer chapel more selectively. The visible light, of what I presume was the Holy Spirit; feeling touched; boldly asking for miraculous healing—these were details that I was certain would make some consider me certifiably insane. I understood how it might seem a bit much. Nonetheless, sometimes I did share the details. At times such conversations ended with an awkward smile from the listener; that was okay. But other times, people felt compelled to share extraordinary things that had happened in their own lives, and that was a blessing.

Hand Bells and Dark Rooms

*C*hristmas was amazing that year. I was attentive in ways I hadn't been in years past. My eyes were open to all around me. The miracle of Christmas seemed pliable, like I could reach out for it and hold it in my hands. I was plugged in and fully engaged. There had been areas in my life where I had slipped into autopilot. One day had rolled into the next; I moved from one chore to another, or from one expectation met to the next one to meet. Before I knew differently, I was sleepwalking through life. This pregnancy, however, had opened my eyes into a wide-awake, "holy cow!" state. God had my attention.

It wasn't my first eyes-wide-open, thank-you-Jesus event. I had been plugged in like this before: Her name was Sophie.

When Sophie was a baby, my friend Katherine asked me to be her personal attendant for her approaching wedding. I was honored. Her mother hosted a luncheon for the girls in her wedding party. We sat at a long oval table inside The River Room, an upscale downtown St. Paul landmark of sorts. Katherine and I had been friends since junior high school. Most of her bridal attendants were also close friends. I knew her family on a first-name, chatty basis. The conversation was light and easy. We gabbed about bridal shops, weepy father/daughter dances, and tacky bridesmaid dresses. During the chit-chat, her mother, Mary Jo, asked me how my Sophie was.

I had so much I needed to say. Not about milestones or bedtimes; instead, I went right for the heart of it. I gushed about how motherhood had changed me, about what an incredible blessing Sophie was in my life. I gushed over how much I adored her. I expressed my astonishment at the unearthing of such intense love for someone—who knew that was possible? I can't remember the words I used to express this overwhelming rush of emotion—with one exception: My last sentence was, "I just can't believe that I get to be her mommy."

I finally stopped talking, realizing I had been rambling on and on about my baby. How annoying that must have been. I looked up and across the table, and much to my surprise, I saw Mary Jo with tears streaming down her face. I was a little taken aback, and I scanned the group, pausing to see Katherine's sister-in-law, Betsy, fanning her face to dry her own tears. She had two young children of her own.

This was a mommy thing. These intense plugged-in moments weren't uniquely mine. The other moms in the room knew just the place I was in. They'd been there too—this place where you're wide-eyed and plugged in, where you can reach out to touch your blessings, pliable in your hands.

Not to say that being plugged in is somehow exclusive to motherhood. It's that place of richness where we find ourselves if we allow the eyes of our heart to truly see. It's why the Christmas I was pregnant with our baby boy was amazing. My heart-eyes were open.

As we sat in church the week before Christmas, I was immersed in all that surrounded me: my husband, strong at my side; my fidgety, beautiful little girl; families who lined the pews, snuggled up tightly against each other; the brisk draft coming from the back of the sanctuary where parishioners trickled in, hoping to go unnoticed; the beauty and warmth of voices singing in unison, praising the miracle of Jesus' birth; the tranquil exquisiteness of the hand bell choir; and the life that I carried within me, knowing that I was touched, and being open to whatever this little one had in store for us—I was plugged into all of it, and it was extraordinary. I experienced the richness of Christmas in a way I hadn't before. I soaked it all in.

Then the holidays passed, the decorations were stored away, and the bitter cold of winter in Minnesota remained. A follow-up ultrasound appointment had been on my calendar, and I was doing my best to ignore it. I was fearful that I might be yanked out of this extraordinary eye-opening place I was in. I had decided I would contest the ultrasound visit. I expressed my concern to my OB-GYN, telling her I didn't want to go back again, that I was fearful they would find something wrong after all.

But she pressed me to go, insisting that there were too many unanswered questions. She convinced me to return, saying that if nothing else, at least it would let us put things to rest, and that we would know for sure. The truth was, though, deep down I already knew for sure: It wasn't over. We had only taken a step back from it. I was working on my courage to face it again. I was working on keeping myself plugged in and aware of God's presence, regardless of the condition of our son's heart.

On a cold, late January morning, we went back to the perinatology clinic—this time, only Paul and I. We wouldn't make the mistake of bringing along a toddler again, not to this office anyway. We were greeted by a different ultrasound technician, someone we hadn't yet met. She ushered us back into the same exam room we had been in when this whole mess started. My very core exuded unease.

The technician started with all her measurements. *Here we go again,* I thought. She tried to lighten the mood with casual small talk, but you could have cut the tension with the proverbial knife. It was draining. She got a profile picture of his sweet little face, commenting on what a great-looking boy he was. She worked at her images diligently, especially when she got to his heart.

Paul asked, "So does his heart look okay to you? Because, you know, there have been some concerns."

The tech didn't respond. Nor would she look up at him, and in that moment we both knew. There was a long pause, like she was working up the courage to say something. It wasn't her place to give us answers, but at the same time, we'd done this before, and when she finally looked up at Paul and said somberly, "Dr. Dawson will need to review the images," we knew what it meant. I knew what I had known all along, but I felt sorry for Paul. Here he was, anguished yet again.

Dr. Dawson entered the room. Coolly, she introduced herself and started looking at the images. She expressed how she was certain that there was a problem with the heart, just as her colleague had initially diagnosed.

I asked her, "Why then did the cardiologist—the one your office sent us to—find nothing wrong?"

She said that she didn't have an answer for me, and that she would like us to see someone else, another cardiologist. Then she called in other technicians to "take a look." They stood huddled together on the other side of the exam table, whispering and pointing at the monitor, while one of them dug the ultrasound wand into my side. The whispering was silly, really, since they were less than two feet away from Paul and me, and we could hear every word. The only thing that was clear was that they had no clue what they were looking at. I'd turned into a "hands on" teaching experience without ever having agreed to be their specimen, and I wished they would stop. They were trying to be polite and as unobtrusive as possible, but it wasn't working. I felt like an attraction, and I was losing the little bit of courage I'd mustered up for this.

As frustration welled up inside me, I asked Dr. Dawson how long it would be before I could get in to see the other cardiologist. When she replied that she thought she could arrange something within the next couple of weeks, I lost it. I had had *enough* with these seemingly well-meaning people, their white coats, their whispering, their obvious limitations, and this cold, dark exam room.

"Frankly," I told her, "there is no way I will wait two more weeks before getting answers."

Did they *know* what this felt like? Not only did I have no control over my circumstance, but I was being pushed around from one doctor to the next, none of whom seemed competent enough to tell my baby's backside from the top of his head! I wanted to scream.

Dr. Dawson could see my building frustration. She left the room without turning her back to me, telling me she'd see if she could get us in earlier.

I was finally able to get off the exam table, and we were brought into a small consultation room behind what looked like the door to any other exam room. Only, inside there was no examination table, no exam gloves, no medical equipment. This room was for other purposes. This was the place to discuss your options, your plans . . . but again with the dim lighting! I understood the need for a darkened room during ultrasounds, but here too? It must have been an attempt at comfort; maybe they think you're less likely to freak out when you're sitting in the dark.

Dr. Dawson offered us an appointment with Dr. Singh, explaining that he was highly experienced and knowledgeable and that she hoped he could give us answers. She said he had offered to come in to see us the first part of next week. Paul and I exchanged a smile. *This just gets more unbelievable.* Dr. Singh was *Blake's* cardiologist. What were the chances? Doug and Brooke were certain that the man could walk on water.

Then Dr. Dawson, without a moment's hesitation, informed us of our other option: We could terminate the pregnancy. So many thoughts rushed through my mind all at once. I guessed this was what a late-term abortion would be, as I was only a week shy of my third trimester. For at least three months now, my ever-expanding abdomen had left no one guessing that I was good and pregnant. My baby commanded much of my petite 5-foot-2-inch frame. I tried to push the gruesome thought of an abortion from my mind.

I felt instinctively protective. I cradled my belly in my hands, embracing the baby. This was my *child*. This was not *the pregnancy*. I was angry. If this were a perfectly healthy baby, termination at this stage of pregnancy would be criminal.

We didn't even know *what* was wrong with him yet— just that *something* was wrong with his heart. I was brokenhearted to know that alone would be considered enough reason to end his life. I was angry that I was put at the helm of this. My emotional state was a train wreck. *I'm given this option— NOW?* Who was I to decide the value of his life? What if I were in a place so dark I couldn't face this? What if I were to panic and want out? Who would protect him? His perceived deficiencies left him defenseless to a world that could easily cast him aside.

The Bracelet

*M*y nights were restless as we waited to meet with Dr. Singh. Fear had a grip on me. I was unplugged again, just as I had feared would happen. I ached for peace again. It had slipped away from me. Maybe I had pushed it away. Maybe there wasn't room, after fear and worry had flooded in to fill my heart. I was broken once more.

After a night of chasing rest, I gave in. I got up and started my day before the sun rose. Paul had slept soundly. I listened in envy to his rhythmic breathing. I peeked in on Sophie, tucked tightly into her bed. She hugged her teddy bear. Her soft dark locks were wild on her pillow.

I walked around in the darkness of my home. I looked out through the picture windows in our living room to find fresh snow blanketing the ground and trees. It glistened as if crystals had been tossed upon the ground. It was incredibly beautiful.

I kneeled in front of the windows, letting moonlight fall onto my shoulders. I asked Jesus, *Where are you? I know you are at my side; I'm certain of it. But the last few days have been difficult. I'm scared, and it's getting harder to feel you here with me. Open my heart to you once again; show me you're still here.* I finished my petition and stayed for a while watching light bounce from the snow crystals.

I was scheduled to work that morning. Exhausted, I did my best to move through the motions of my day. I had finished college while I was pregnant with Sophie. Now I worked for a small, private dental practice as a dental hygienist—a good fit for me; it suited my chatty, social nature. The staff was close-knit and family-like. My co-workers were well aware of all that had gone on during my pregnancy.

I called my obstetrician that morning. When she returned my call, I excused myself from my patient and hurried into a private room. She listened as I poured out all my frustrations to her. I told her how upsetting it had been to have all those people file into the ultrasound room, wanting to "take a peek," and all the while, no one seemed competent enough to make a diagnosis. I told her how cold Dr. Dawson had seemed and how she had rubbed me the wrong way. I expressed to her how I wished they wouldn't have kept speculating over the diagnosis. Their speculations had filled my head with useless noise and worry. I told her that when I had finally had enough, I had tuned them out and started to hear their voices the way Charlie Brown heard adults in *Peanuts* specials on TV.

"Wait a minute, what?" she asked. Maybe sharing the *Peanuts* thing was a bit much.

She let me say everything I wanted to. When I finished, she offered to help me, as much as she could, to make sense of this. And she told me she was sorry—about all of it.

I hung up the receiver and sat for a moment. I was grateful for her kindness, but it hadn't made me feel less alone. I thought about that morning before the sun rose, petitioning Jesus to show himself to me.

I started to make my way back to my waiting patient, when I was stopped by my co-worker Tina. With tears in her eyes, she grabbed for my arm, telling me that she had something for me. She lifted my hand and slipped a bracelet onto my wrist. It was a silver bangle, well worn, and encircled with an inscription. It took me a moment to read it, as some of the letters had worn smooth into the silver. It said: "With God all things are possible. Matthew 19:26." My eyes widened in disbelief, and I immediately felt flushed and warm. I asked, "Where did this come from?" She smiled and said that the patient in her room gave it to her . . . to give to me. I asked, "Just now?"

"Yes, just now." she replied. "It was the coolest thing. I noticed it and asked her where I could buy one like it. I told her that it would mean a lot to a friend right now. She pulled it off her wrist and handed it to me, telling me that she wanted me to have it. She said, "If you think it would mean a lot to your friend, then I want you to give her this one." Tina and I looked at each other, smiling. Then she said, "You wanna hear the best part? She said she hasn't worn this bracelet in months. For some reason, this morning she knew she had to wear it, that there would be a reason for her to."

I had asked Jesus to show himself to me, and he responded—with jewelry!

I wore the bracelet every day. Each time I looked at it, it made me smile. It was a tangible reminder of God's presence. Paul teased me, saying if I continued to question God's presence, he would surely show up at our bedside, white flowing robe and all. But I didn't need that. With the bracelet encircling my wrist, I felt cherished, and throughout the rest of my pregnancy, I never again doubted his presence.

Part III

He Whispers

Jesus said, "Let the little children come to me, and do not hinder them, for the kingdom of heaven belongs to such as these." —Matthew 19:14 (New International Version)

I lay in my hospital bed, broken.

After a traumatic few hours following our baby's birth, Paul and I left Children's Hospital and returned to Abbott Northwestern. My personal belongings were moved, and I was placed on an entirely new floor, a high-risk maternity floor. I was annoyed.

She came into my room and made herself comfortable, sitting with legs crossed on the empty bed next to mine. Clipped to her blouse was a hospital ID badge. She was young and brunette. She wore a sleek pencil skirt and cute black pumps. A hospital coordinator, assigned to facilitate high-risk cases like mine, she asked, "How are things going? Is there anything we can do for you?" I was agitated, my patience ice-thin. What could she do for us? Why was she smiling and sitting on the bed?

So I asked her—snippily, I'm afraid—"I don't understand why I was moved. Why am I on *this* floor?" She responded by saying that this too was a maternity floor, and that the staff here can take care of my needs. Fine, but I pressed on because she still hadn't answered my question. "Okay, but why did I need to be moved *here*?" Finally, she gave me a docile little smile, the kind tainted with pity. I had seen it before.

"Well, we thought you might be more comfortable here . . . away from the babies." Ah, now I understood perfectly. *Am I so twisted that I am incapable of sharing space with women with healthy babies?* I was insulted, and yet I realized that she, with the badge and the cute shoes, was right. I was ashamed of the envy and the resentment I felt toward the mothers I had watched leaving the hospital with their healthy new babies that morning.

I lay there in my new hospital room, longing for rest. My body ached with exhaustion, yet my mind swirled around my little boy. I felt guilty for leaving his bedside. Did he know we weren't there? His nurse had pressed us to go back to Abbott to rest. We had given in grudgingly. There was nothing we could do for him, and that was the hardest part. I couldn't even hold him.

The nurse had assured us that he wasn't in pain. They were keeping him heavily sedated and highly medicated to let his little body recover. I recognized this about his *body*, the *physical* part of him . . . but where *was* he? Where was his little *person*? Did he know that we were here, desperately needing and loving him? Did he know that he had a big sister who had waited patiently for his arrival and who couldn't wait to meet him?

It was a cruel entry into the world. All he had ever known was the warmth and protection of my womb. Then, in an instant of time, he had been thrust into the cold, having to fight for each breath. Was he still cold? Was he lonely?

I asked Jesus to hold him for me. I asked him to scoop my baby into his arms so that he would be warmed and loved. I imagined Jesus standing by our son's Isolette, showering him with all he needed. He would lack nothing; he would not feel abandoned or alone.

I lay in my own pain, listening to a woman next door in hers. She was in labor, high-risk labor. Maybe her labor had come too soon, or maybe her baby was already gone and still she labored. Her moaning and groaning went on and on. There was physical pain, but I heard more in her cries. Grief covered her. I never saw her face, and yet I was connected to her pain. The hallway was silent. No team of doctors and nurses waited to whisk her baby away. There was no chaos. I heard no newborn cries—only stillness. I prayed that Jesus would find her, that he would cradle her in her pain too.

The morning came and we anxiously made our way over to Children's. I missed my baby so and needed to be close to him. I studied every little thing about him, just as I had done when Sophie was brand new. He was handsome and sweet. This time there was so much more to wrap my mind around. I wanted to understand all the lines that came from different parts of his body. I wanted to know about the monitors and instruments that surrounded him. I noticed that he had more equipment around him than the other babies he shared this wing with.

It took time for us to figure out where we belonged, to find our place, our footing, here. The staff educated us gently. They discussed NICU etiquette in regard to other babies and families. They explained the need for discretion in this open wing. We needed to imagine that each baby's area was private, as if they all occupied separate rooms.

We respected other families' privacy the best we could as we spent hours in this wing each day. We did our best to look away from micro-preemies that fit into the palm of a hand. But their images stick with you, even if you only catch a glimpse of them. Their underdeveloped nervous systems cause their tiny bodies to shake. Their skin was translucent; still, they were beautiful.

Likewise, I am sure others did their best to look away from our baby. Most infants in the NICU are tiny. Our son was full-term at delivery. He had not been weighed during the chaos following his birth, but his birth weight was guessed to have been about eight pounds. He was puffy as he recovered from surgery. The edema made him look like a little sumo wrestler. His swollen body nearly took up the entire Isolette. Parents tried not to hold their gaze, but their faces were full of questions.

As I sat at his bedside, I thought about his nursery at home. It was a small bedroom nestled close to our own. We had worked at making it just right. Already it smelled like baby lotion and fresh, clean linen.

The perfect nursery—it had seemed as important as finding the right OB-GYN, or staying up until midnight discussing baby names with your husband. You've imagined the two of you together in this sweet room. You've anticipated two a.m. feedings, the rest of the world snuggled in their beds.

I had become obsessed during my first pregnancy with finding just the right shade of lilac to paint the nursery walls. Once I found it, I searched all over for the perfect coordinated bedding and accessories. Then there were the window treatments. I dragged my sister-in-law into countless fabric stores to help me find just the right color combination.

Our baby boy's room had a safari animal theme. Paul had painted the walls in a rich blue and apple green. Less energy was put into his room than had been put into Sophie's. It was just as sweet, but it lacked the obsessive details I had poured into hers. I guess this time, with all that had transpired as we waited on him, the perfect little room seemed insignificant. Things were different emotionally as well—even thorny.

Compared to the nursery that awaited our little one at home, the hospital was sterile and cold. The linens were unisex. Nothing distinguished a baby boy from a baby girl. There were only sick babies. It wasn't the warm place I'd imagined holding and rocking my baby in the middle of the night.

Nevertheless, there was something amazing here. When I let my anger and disappointment melt away, that's when I could see him: Amid the white coats, the tiny breathing tubes, and the brokenhearted, exhausted parents, there was a heavenly presence. *Jesus* held these babies close. He was not restricted by IVs and monitors. He was not restricted by illness. They were warmed in his presence. His strong hands cradled the tiniest ones. He whispered words of admiration into their ears. This wasn't the perfectly decorated nursery of my mind's eye; this was something more.

Above each child's area was a computer-generated sign with a soft pastel cartoon image of a cute little animal. Above each image, the baby's name was displayed in soft bubble lettering. Each sign was unique—countless different animals. Ours had a sweet fat brown bear wearing farmer's overalls. The pastel bubble lettering said "Charlie."

An Ugly Dagger

Charlie's neonatologist came by to check in on us. She was the doctor who had run with Paul through the tunnel system. Her appearance was soft: long, gray hair that spiraled down past her face in perfect natural ringlets; fair skin; pretty, blue eyes. Yet, there was a distinguished presence about her, and her communication was oh-so-direct. She explained that Charlie's body was working hard to recover from all he had gone through the day before. She described his ordeal as a "great insult on his tiny body." She said his resuscitation was the most difficult they'd seen here in quite some time. Then she startled me by making reference to a stroke. "What stroke?" I asked in a panic. *What is she talking about?*

She broke the news to me in a coldly detached tone, as if speaking of someone else's child. He had suffered a stroke on the day of his birth. They weren't sure when it happened—during his resuscitation or his septostomy. She said there was a pool of blood on the left side of his brain. She tried to offer some reassurance, explaining that it was contained within a certain lobe of his brain, and chances were that it wouldn't affect his cognitive ability or speech. However, only time would tell. She explained that any lasting effects would be seen on the right side of his body, that he might not have full muscular strength on that side. The panic escalated inside me. I wanted Paul . . .

He had left the hospital for only an hour or so, at my insistence. He had been squirrelly, as if the hospital walls were closing in on him. Fortunately, my mom was with me, and I asked her to call him and tell him to come back. Wanting to hide away, I made my way to a lactation room.

Down a quiet hallway the little rooms were lined up, one after another. A small plaque outside each said "Nursing Mother Room." Each had a comfortable chair and a radio set to soft music. The rooms were dimly lit. I fell into one of them and locked the door behind me. I sat and started the monotonous practice of expressing milk. I longed to have Charlie at my breast instead.

I shut my eyes, and the repetitive swooshing sound of the breast pump started. My center began to calm. I imagined Charlie as a young boy, frail and thin. His gait was unbalanced, and he held his wasted right arm close to his side. I wanted to protect him. I thought about Sophie. I had never valued her strong personality the way I did in that moment. She was opinionated, sassy, and smart. I imagined her as a protector, an additional caregiver of sorts. I imagined us surrounding Charlie in love and protection.

Paul called to me from the hallway, and then there was a small tap on the door. In my disheveled state, I opened it slightly, and he slid through. Fear showed all over his face. He urgently asked me what had happened—*was Charlie okay?*—and dropped to his knees in front of where I sat in the rocking chair. I said that he was, hearing my own words as a lie falling from my lips. But, I told him, a CT scan had revealed that our boy had suffered a stroke. The word *stroke* came from my mouth like a dagger, ugly and hurtful. I hadn't intended for my tone to be so dark. I had little control.

Up until that moment, my crying within these walls had been quiet and polite. But now I cried out loudly. My weeping was an audible reflection of my pain. Paul held me tightly, and we wept together.

It haunted me when I reflected upon how easily we could have lost him at birth. Nothing had gone the way we imagined.

Jeopardy! and Other Games

Our first meeting with Dr. Singh, weeks prior to Charlie's birth

When the snow is fresh and clean, and the cold isn't unbearable, winter in Minnesota holds a certain magic. Looking out into a crisp day can easily place your imagination right inside a Norman Rockwell painting. As a little girl, I spent hours playing outside in the mountains of snow. I carved little snow caves, imagining my life as an Eskimo. I stayed out as long as I could, crispness nestled into my lungs. In time, the exposed place between my jacket sleeve and my mitten would get the best of me. I retreated back into the warm house, with numb, tingling wrists and frosty cheeks.

As a grown-up, you start noticing that winter days look different, a bit less picturesque. They can be messy and dirty, especially on busy city streets. Grime, salt, and sand mixes with melting snow and is catapulted up onto street corners by passing traffic. It is an unsightly, un-Rockwellian, sloppy mess that leaves you eager for a fresh dusting of white.

My life these past weeks seemed to parallel the grimy mess of winter city streets. It seemed fitting that it was a dreary January morning when we headed off to meet for the first time with Dr. Singh. He agreed to see us at the perinatology clinic—in the same office where Dr. Dawson keeps her ego. We drove over the Mississippi River on the Wabasha

Street Bridge, heading toward the clinic near downtown St. Paul. I looked out the window as we passed through a run-down neighborhood in this otherwise charming old city. All the while, I assessed the need for a fresh snowfall. A little sunshine would be nice too.

We pulled into the mucky parking garage and started our ascent through the ramp. As we searched for a parking spot, we caught a glimpse of an immaculately dressed, though not ostentatious, man. "Look, I bet that's him," Paul said, as if we had just spotted a celebrity. We watched him rush toward the building, heightening my anxiety about making it to our appointment on time. Paul pulled into a parking spot, and just as we got out of the car, my cell phone rang. It was the clinic, asking if we were on our way and informing us that Dr. Singh had arrived. We weren't even late yet! I started then to appreciate what a big deal Dr. Singh must be.

We made our way inside, skipping the waiting room routine as an ultrasound technician was waiting to usher us back. She started with her images, and easy chit-chat ensued. Her name was Pam. She was kind and soft-spoken. She asked if we'd met Dr. Singh yet. We told her we hadn't, but that we'd heard only good things. We chatted about Blake and how Doug and Brooke had wonderful things to say about Dr. Singh.

She looked up and said, "He is wonderful. He was my son's cardiologist too." A bit taken aback, I quickly asked how her son was doing now.

"He passed away in infancy," Pam said. Looking at me, and sensing my unease, she added softly, "He would be eighteen years old now, and so much has changed in the last few years." She smiled and said, "The first time I saw Dr. Singh here at the clinic, years had passed since my son's death, and he recognized me right away. He asked about my family. He is a very special man."

Pam asked if it would be okay if a couple of other people came in to observe. "Sure," I said. I mean, what's the difference anymore? At least she had asked for my permission, and she was incredibly kind.

They filed in, and it started to feel like we were on a game show. Not the *Let's Make a Deal* kind with clowns and fat suits; no, the more serious, studious type, like *Jeopardy!* They took turns looking over each other's shoulders and talking things through, except that it seemed they had more questions than answers. Dr. Dawson was there too. I sat with my belly exposed and wondered where Dr. Singh was. Isn't he the expert? I bet he'll have more answers than questions. Then it dawned on me that, in game-show fashion, they were trying to come up with the right answer before bringing Dr. Singh in.

One last technician made her way around the end of the bed to the ultrasound machine. She smiled at me and asked how I was doing today. I smiled and lied, saying, "I'm fine, thank you." She was much older than the rest. Her figure was round, as were her soft pink cheeks. She reached for her readers dangling from a cord around her neck. She wore a nametag pinned to her lab coat; it read "Margaret." The others backed away from her slightly as if they expected her to have the answer, and they wanted to give space for it. She spent only moments peering at the screen through her glasses positioned on the tip of her nose. She was quiet as she looked. The others whispered their thoughts to her, and then waited for validation. She didn't respond.

After a moment of silence, she said, "This is Transposition of the Great Arteries." She said it without hesitation and without the inflection of a question in her voice. She then pointed out the pertinent landmarks to the rest of them. Paul and I watched the faces of the others. It became clear now, the way a mind-teasing puzzle does: impossible at first, but once you've got the answer, you can't believe it's been sitting there in front of you the whole time.

Dr. Dawson looked annoyed, as she had just been shown up by an ultrasound technician with decades more experience. She stepped out of the room to let Dr. Singh know we were ready, and the others, with the exception of Margaret, filed behind.

Dr. Singh knocked politely and then came into the room. He smiled at us warmly and introduced himself, extending his hand. He was probably nearing sixty years of age and was of Indian descent. What little remained of his accent was distant in his speech. He was slender. He had thinning salt-and-pepper hair and a neatly trimmed beard. His facial features were strong. He was handsome, an attribute I hadn't anticipated.

Returning his warm smile and greeting, we expressed how nice it was to finally meet him. "A patient of yours is our godson, and to say you came highly recommended would be an understatement," I said.

I shared Blake's name and Dr. Singh's face lit up with both puzzlement and delight. He said, "Well, I can honestly say that in all my years of doing this, I don't think I have ever had that happen before." He added with a smile, "I don't know that I'm the kind of guy you want to have to refer a friend to."

He came around to the side of the table where the ultra-sound machine sat. He asked Margaret for images, and the two of them worked quietly together. After a few minutes, they left the room, giving Paul and me a moment alone. I got down from the bed and cleaned the jelly mess from my belly. The lights were still turned down. We chatted about how genuine Dr. Singh seemed, and how impressive Margaret was. We also remarked at the consistency of Dr. Dawson's ugly bedside manner.

Dr. Singh knocked softly on the door to signal his return. He came into the room and leaned up against the bed. He was physically closer to me than I remember a doctor ever being before. I appreciated his intimacy. He made sure he had my gaze and said softly, "It looks like your baby has a condition known as Transposition of the Great Arteries."

He then explained that our little one's aorta artery and pulmonary artery were transposed, which would prevent oxygen-rich blood from reaching his body following birth. Dr. Singh explained further that Charlie's growth and development in utero was normal because I was providing him with oxygen. But, he stated, "Your baby will need heart surgery to correct the condition before he can leave the hospital."

Dr. Singh shared a time line, and told us that in some cases, babies with Transposition need two surgical procedures: one prior to open-heart surgery, known as a septostomy, to create a hole between his heart chambers and allow him to get oxygen to his body until the open-heart surgery could be performed. He explained it as a temporary fix.

A bit of my own heart broke away as I realized I couldn't protect my baby from this.

Then Dr. Singh told us that the positive thing about Transposition is that once you're ready to leave the hospital, you're leaving with a relatively healthy baby. He said that although the defect is complex and rare, it's one that they've effectively corrected over the past twenty years. He smiled and said, "My oldest Transposition survivor, who had the same surgery we will perform on your son, is now nineteen. She has a full life. She just started college."

Yet, his word survivor struck me. To be one meant you had faced some great challenge. It felt like a boulder now lay in our baby's path. So I guess this is it, I thought. Things have been easy for us. We've been happy. We've been healthy. We are in a good marriage. We are blessed with a smart, beautiful little girl. This must be "the other shoe," as they say.

"So what will happen after he's born?" I asked, as the logistics started to flood my mind. Dr. Singh explained that a team of doctors and nurses from the NICU at Children's Hospital would be present at his birth. He said, "You will be able to hold him for a bit, then you'll hand him over to the NICU team. They will make sure he's stable, and then an echocardiogram will be done to confirm his diagnosis." Dr. Singh asked me where I planned to deliver the baby. I told him that our OB typically delivers at United Hospital, here in St. Paul.

"So, what will happen if we are here in St. Paul?" I asked.

"Well, the baby will need to be transported by ambulance over to the Minneapolis Children's Campus, and your husband will need to join him." So, my ill son and my husband will be across town, while I am left here in St. Paul? His words led me to the obvious.

"Wouldn't it make more sense if I delivered him in Minneapolis?" I asked.

He didn't respond right away, instead turning a bit to look over his shoulder. He leaned in closer to us and, lowering his voice, said, "I don't want to step on anybody's toes here, but, yes, it would be best if you delivered at Abbott."

Without a moment's pause, I said, "Well, then, that is just what we'll do."

Paul and I gave our warmest thanks, and Dr. Singh expressed to us how sorry he was for our news. He also expressed that he would be there to help us get through this.

Dr. Dawson returned to the room just as Dr. Singh was leaving. She tried to run through some of the details with us. "Once the baby is stable, we will transport him over to Children's in Minneapolis," she said. I returned her cool, matter-of-fact tone as I told her that we had decided it would be best to deliver the baby at Abbott rather than United.

All of my intuition about this woman came to light before my eyes. She started out by saying, "Well, you know, your OB doesn't have privileges at Abbott, and that will mean having to find a new doctor who does. You may find yourself in a sticky insurance situation." I was thrown by her snippy tone. She sounded like an angry child. She continued her rant: "I assure you that the staff at Children's here in St. Paul is quite capable of stabilizing and caring for your son. Up until just the past couple of years, heart surgeries were performed at both campuses. We can stabilize and care for him here, and then have him transported before surgery. It's only a twenty-minute ambulance ride across town."

"And what about me?" I asked. My baby and I were being manipulated into a situation for the benefit of a hospital, or, worse yet, to stroke this unpleasant woman's ego by allowing her to oversee our care. "I'll be here recovering, while my baby and husband are across town?" I questioned back, returning her snippy tone.

"Yes," she said. "But we aren't anticipating the need for a cesarean birth, so we could get you over there within a couple of days." The harsh condescension in her voice made my pulse quicken.

"What happens if for some reason I need a cesarean, and then I am away from him for days? Besides, isn't it best to have his cardiologist across the street rather than across town?"

She continued to push, saying that usually babies with Transposition are okay during their first forty-eight hours or so. I wondered if she would take this chance with her own child. What would happen if he needed surgery immediately? Why did this seem like common sense to me, the one without the medical degree?

Mindy Lynn

I looked her straight in the eye, and told her a second and final time, "I will deliver this baby at Abbott rather than at United, because that is what's best."

She turned away from us and left the room. It was the last time I ever spoke to her. Although I returned to the clinic countless times for additional ultrasounds and tests, I made it clear to her staff that I no longer needed her "counsel."

Throwing Fruit

The days following Charlie's birth were so emotionally draining, so taxing, that I found it impossible to cover all my ugly. It seemed as though once I had reached a tipping point, my relationship rules, the manner in which I chose to express myself, were simply chucked. Chucked—the same way you pitch a sticky, wet apple core out the driver's window of your vehicle. It's swift and intentional, because you can't continue to hold the sticky mess.

It was about to get sticky with my father-in-law; I couldn't hold on to it any longer.

My father-in-law is a man I respect. He worked endlessly and selflessly to provide opportunity for his family. He was driven in part, I'm sure, by his poverty-stricken childhood. The tragedy of the Armenian Massacres during World War I left his family forever changed. His once proud, wealthy family had been victimized in ways difficult to imagine: genocide. While there is no clear consensus to the number of Armenian souls lost, most western scholars have agreed on an estimated 1.5 million. Those who escaped the massacres and death camps were driven out of their homes and stripped of all material wealth. Many survivors settled throughout the Middle East. Hitler would later look to the atrocities of the Armenian genocide as a playbook of sorts. Much of his approach of eradicating the Jews was based on the torment of the Armenians thirty years earlier.

Paul's grandfather, just a year old, survived. He was hidden away in a cellar during the killing of men and male children. Survivors traveled by caravan, walking through the Syrian Desert. After months of travel, they found solace and safety in Western Syria. Paul's great-grandmother survived the pilgrimage, but found herself unable to care for her children. She was forced to leave Paul's grandfather in an orphanage run by Catholic Charities.

Heart-wrenching stories of survival and loss no doubt shaped my father-in-law's youth. The family had very little. Armenian survivors lived and worked together. They found a new place for themselves, forming Christian neighborhoods in the predominantly Muslim country.

My father-in-law was sent away to seminary as a young boy. He took advantage of the education it provided, soaking up the study of languages. Yet he left prematurely, for reasons he has never expressed, and returned home, fluent in Armenian, Arabic, and French; other languages would come later. He found work selling pharmaceuticals and, just barely out of his teens, became the provider for his family. He moved his parents and brothers from the one-room home he grew up in into his own home, with his wife and children.

He assumed the position of family patriarch, as was customary of the eldest son. He provided well for his family; his children wanted for nothing—which was vastly different from his own childhood. He adored his wife and his mother, and worked incessantly to provide them with the things they wanted. There was live-in help, beautiful home furnishings, and travel. Paul, his mother, his brothers, and their nanny would pack up for the summers and head to Beirut. My father-in-law would stay behind—to work, of course.

He started their paperwork years in advance—paperwork that would allow his sons to immigrate to the United States. It was a continuation of the pilgrimage that had started sixty years earlier in Armenia. Being torn from their homes had been beyond their control, while this pilgrimage was by choice and with intent. I imagine there was a sense of power in that. My father-in-law—I say this respectfully—had an affinity for regulating circumstance.

And . . . here we go.

I sat resting in my hospital bed at Abbott. The phone next to my bed rang—my father calling from Texas. He was upset and struggled to express himself. Our relationship had always lacked time, but never affection. My parents divorced when I was five, and my dad and I lived 1500 miles apart. I didn't know the details, like what his favorite TV show was, or how he liked his eggs. Yet, there was always warmth whenever we picked up the phone. It was easy.

Now, however, he was having a hard time as he nervously asked how Charlie was doing, and how we were. I started to recount the chaotic hours after Charlie's birth, and with each detail, my dad grew more verbally withdrawn. He simply had no words.

As our conversation progressed, my father-in-law, Jack, entered the room and sat down in a chair at the end of my bed. He was immaculately dressed in a full suit, hat, and tie; he rarely dressed in anything else. He wore his hospital and clinic badges clipped to his jacket lapel, his name printed across them with the title "Interpreter" in bold letters. His arrival during my phone conversation lessened the pressure of breaking the latest news to him; as it happened, I informed my father and my father-in-law at the same time that Charlie had suffered a stroke. I repeated the details that we had learned that day (that time would tell the extent of the damage, that it shouldn't affect his cognitive ability, but that he might not have full function of his right side). I shared medical details I knew were inconsequential to my father but which I knew my medically minded father-in-law would appreciate.

Finally, my father told me he loved me and we said our goodbyes. I hung up the phone, knowing this conversation had only just begun.

Paul's father sat looking indifferent, as if he'd already been told this news. He started off by expressing that this is just a little bit of blood in his head. It will dissipate, he said, and it wasn't really a *stroke*. I could feel anger welling up inside of me. I knew I didn't have the capacity to stuff it away, not today. This was likely to get a bit ugly. He was patronizing me. He was trying to downplay the situation in an attempt to somehow "save me." I had seen it before in this family, and it infuriated me. This time he was trying to do it to *me*.

I was still angry about the fact that Paul's grandmother had been left in the dark about the whole situation with Charlie. She was being "saved." She was in Beirut, so hiding it from her was quite easy. Beirut was her home, but in recent years she had spent months at a time visiting my mother-in-law in the States. I adored her, and she adored me. She always smiled when I walked into a room and would then say, in Arabic, that I was "sweet, like a peach."

She had survived unthinkable heartbreak in her young adult life. She was only twenty-nine years old when her husband was killed in a car accident, leaving her with five young children. He had owned a successful tailoring business. Prior to the accident, her life was pampered. The accident changed everything. Her youngest two children were taken from her by her childless brother and sister-in-law, who claimed she couldn't care for all of the children on her own. They also took her husband's tailoring business.

She spent the following five years in court trying to get her life back. She eventually reclaimed her business, but she never got her youngest children back. Relationships had grown sour, and she wasn't allowed to see them. As a young widow in the Middle East, she had no power.

The tragedy she endured wasn't the amazing part of her story. The amazing, beautiful part of her story was how she faced her darkness. It hadn't consumed her; it didn't define who she was. Instead, her faith defined her. I'm certain that she had dark moments, but darkness wasn't a place where she let herself get comfortable. She relied on prayer. Each day at one o'clock, she sat and prayed for an hour. She recited the Hail Mary over and over. If you happened to walk in on her daily ritual, she would smile at you from across the room and continue on. She was known within the family for having a special way with prayer. Practice makes perfect.

The whole point is, she was somewhat of a prayer warrior, and I needed her. *We* needed her. I had asked repeatedly throughout my pregnancy if anyone had told her. I was always given the same answer: no. They didn't want to upset her; they weren't sure if she could "handle it." I was increasingly angry about it. Paul said that it was a cultural thing, and I could clearly see that he was right. Still, it annoyed him too.

Important doctor visits in the *old country* would end with the doctor discussing the diagnosis with the eldest male of the family, not necessarily the patient. The doctor would leave it up to the (male) family members to tell the patient what they thought was best. Whether it was truthful or not was inconsequential. Women were treated like children in an attempt to "protect" or "save" them from life's painful realities. And now, here I was, and my father-in-law was trying to do it to me. *Well, not today. This is America, Jack. Women of my generation, in this country, are taught to be independent and strong. We are encouraged to educate ourselves, and we insist on intellectual equality and respect.*

For the first time in our relationship, I didn't choose to just accept it and smile. Instead, I fired back. I told Jack that he didn't know the first thing about it because he simply wasn't there. I pointed out that he hadn't talked with any doctors, but that I had, because I was Charlie's mother. I told him that he was insulting my intelligence. I told him that I understood what a stroke is, thank you very much. "I am not only in the know," I said, "I *am* the know." There it was, the sticky mess, officially chucked.

I wish I could say that it made me feel better, but it only left me feeling crazy. This line had needed to be drawn, no doubt about it, but doing so didn't bring any sense of satisfaction. There was no *Ah, that felt good*, in part because, looking over at him, I saw pain and fear. His own son, Paul, was hurting, and there was no way for him to make it better. Jack's position in his family, his position in his community, his knowledge of medicine—none of it mattered right now. None of it helped, so he was simply doing the one thing he could do: He was trying to "save us," and I had just made it impossible for him. He was powerless, and I felt empty.

My second and last night at Abbott I lay awake trying to digest the new reality. My baby had suffered a *stroke*. Strokes were something that happened to old men who drank whiskey and carried Lucky Strikes in their shirt pockets. It was like my son had been placed fifty yards behind the starting line; he'd been knocked down and yet was still expected to get up and run. And I was at the sidelines, yelling, "It's not fair! But it's not fair!"

Besides the emotional hurt, I was in a great deal of physical pain. Any little movement in bed sent shooting pain through my pelvis. I hadn't given my body an opportunity to recover from childbirth, instead standing at the side of Charlie's Isolette much of the day. Now I lay there in pain, wondering why the Vicodin the nurse had given me didn't seem to help.

I would be discharged from the hospital in the morning. I was angry that there were no exceptions made for women in my situation. I felt like I had given birth ten minutes ago. I knew that being discharged simply meant gathering my things and being wheeled through the tunnel system to Children's. There would be no recovery. How would I function when I was so physically exhausted?

I looked over at the phone, fearful that it might ring. *What if it's about Charlie? What if his heart rate starts to drop again? What if it starts to race again? What if the bleeding in his brain starts again? What if he never walks, or talks? And what is going to happen to our baby girl? How will she handle being **his** big sister?* It seemed like so much to ask of her, still in pigtails. *Does she need me now? What if we never bring him home? What if we have to leave him here, cold?* I was still staring at the phone, willing it not to ring. *Where are my convictions that everything will be okay?*

I started to search for the nurse call button as the room began to spin. The spinning came on with no advance notice and at an incredible speed. It felt like I was in the center of a merry-go-round, the old-fashioned kind that started to disappear from playgrounds when I was a child. It was like I started off in the center, but the spinning was so intense I slipped part-way out, where it's harder to hold on. The pressure was great. I felt tempted to just let go where I knew I would be thrown from it completely. I was scared to hold onto the cold, dirty aluminum, and I was scared to let go and allow myself to escape into the darkness. It felt like the darkness was calling.

The nurse appeared at my bedside and asked what I needed. I told her that I felt like I was going to pass out. I told her that the room was spinning around me. She turned on all of the lights, making me feel like a lab specimen. She brought my bed to an upright position and checked my vitals. She then resorted to standing just inches away and staring. She thought that maybe the Vicodin was a bit much for me. I expressed to her that I never take medication of any sort, and yes, it probably was a bit much.

The next words just leapt out, without a second of conscious thought. I said, "My head just feels so heavy, and I feel like I *want* to pass out, like it would feel good somehow." I heard myself, and I felt like I was tiptoeing into the dark. Her first response was, "Honey, trust me, you don't want to pass out, 'cause then there will be a whole mess of people in here." Then she said to me with tender eyes, "I understand that you got some unexpected news today about your son. I'm very sorry." Since Charlie and I were at different hospitals, I hadn't considered that they would communicate such things. I felt regret for letting my flirtation with the dark slip out, but the kind nurse stayed and chatted for a while, and I started to feel a bit more like myself.

The spinning finally stopped. I tried hard to clear my mind and allow myself to sleep. I knew I was in terrible need of rest. Instead I thought about what an exhausting pregnancy it had been, with little time for reflection. As one whirlwind of confusion and upset abruptly ended, instantly, I had found myself in a bigger storm.

I started to envision how different things would have been if we had been given miraculous healing. I would have been on a regular maternity floor, where soft pink babies are free of ventilators and tubes. I would have my baby at my chest, skin to skin, learning the contour of his face. He would be perfect in every way. It's what I longed for now.

Even in this dark moment, and in my longing for something different, I found it impossible to deny God's presence. Yet, I desired more than his *presence*. I wanted *healing*—the kind that people would talk about for years; healing that causes faithless, godless doctors to pause for a moment; the kind that makes some nurses simply smile because, for them, miraculous healing is perfectly reasonable.

Waiting

But those who wait on the LORD shall renew their strength; They shall mount up with wings like eagles, They shall run and not be weary, They shall walk and not faint. —Isaiah 40:31 (New King James Version)

"Mommy, Mommy, he finally cracked out?" Sophie asked over the phone.

"Yes, honey, he finally cracked out. You are a big sister," I replied.

We were close to Easter, so her little world was full of pastel eggs and chocolate bunnies. One day leading up to Charlie's delivery, I had seen the gears turning in her sweet head. As she stared at my very full, very round belly, she said, "Mommy, your belly looks like a great big egg . . . So that's how it works! He's gonna get bigger and bigger, until one day he'll just crack out of there!" She was certain she had the answer. She never asked me for confirmation. Since she was so young, I was happy she hadn't, and I never volunteered anything else.

"When do I get to come and see him, Mommy?" she asked.

"Maybe Teta"—"Grandma" in Arabic—"can bring you tomorrow. Mommy misses you, Sophie, very much." Then I approached the difficult news. "Sophie, honey, do you remember when Mommy told you that baby Charlie might be born a little sick?"

"Yes, is he sick?" she questioned.

"Yes, hun, he is. But he has lots of nurses and doctors to help him get better. When you pray at night at Teta's house, I want you to pray that your baby Charlie gets better and better, okay?"

"Okay, Mommy, I will. When are you coming home?" she asked.

"Mommy and Daddy need to be with your brother while he gets better. You get to spend time at Teta's house, okay? He needs to get better before we can bring him home."

"Okay, Mom," she said reluctantly. Her tone weighed heavily on my heart. "I can't wait for him to get better and come home, so then he can turn into a baby girl."

"What, honey?" I asked, sure I had misunderstood.

"I *said*," she replied, "I can't wait until he comes home, so he can turn into a *baby girl!*" She said "baby girl" nice and loud, ensuring that I wouldn't ask "What?" again. I started to chuckle. I was blessed by this little firecracker. She was exactly what my heart needed. I felt comfortable letting her believe that her baby brother "cracked out of there." But I couldn't let her go on believing that he would magically turn into the sister of her dreams just as soon as we got home. This one I needed to address, so we had a little discussion about how Charlie was born her baby brother, and how he would stay her baby brother. She listened to my explanation, but I got the clear sense that she was thinking, *Hmm, just wait and see, Mom, it'll be magic.*

So Sophie continued to spend time with her Teta, waiting on her "brother," and for the life she imagined. She had waited all this time for his arrival, and now she was asked to wait some more. We were asking so much of her. Her little world was upside down.

I asked more of Charlie too. We were three days past his birth, and he was still alarmingly unstable. The nurses gave Paul and me a pager to keep with us at all times. If we left the NICU, they needed to know where we were. We both knew the reason, but we never discussed it, not with the staff, not with each other. As Charlie lay in his Isolette, every few moments a different bell or alarm from a monitor would go off, prompting his nurse to adjust this or that. It was an orchestrated three-ring circus to keep him alive. It filled me with anxiety. He had multiple IVs coming from each limb and running in every direction.

Standing by his bedside, fearful, I waited for his nurse to step away. When she did, I bent down close to his Isolette and started to whisper in his ear. Riddled with guilt, I selfishly asked him for more. I told him that I was sorry this had happened to him. I told him that I loved him more than anything. I told him that I wished I could make it better, that I would do anything to scoop him up in my arms. I asked him to fight harder for his mommy, because I needed him. I told him that I knew he must be really tired, but he had to keep fighting, he couldn't give up. I told him that I had this wonderful life waiting for him. Then his nurse returned, and I walked away feeling ashamed.

I retreated to one of the family lounges, sank into a sofa, and scanned the room. Sofas, recliners, TV, phone, refrigerator, exhausted faces, and one precious, healthy little girl. She was new on her feet, resembling a Weeble Wobble toy. She had thin, silky blonde hair that formed perfect soft ringlets adorning her head like a princess's crown. She was clearly very attached to her sippy cup; each time it fell from her hands, she struggled toward it to pick it up again. She was with her grandmother, a middle-aged woman in a long jean skirt who had long gray-blonde hair neatly pinned up in a bun at the base of her neck.

This beautiful little girl reminded me of Sophie at her age, determined and strong. "She's precious," I said to the woman. "What's her name?"

"Thank you. This is Madison. It's been a challenge to keep her occupied in here. I am afraid she hasn't slept much, and it's starting to affect us all," she said, with a smile.

"Your granddaughter?" I questioned.

"Yes," she replied.

We spent the next few minutes chatting on the sofa as Madison explored the room. I asked about the circumstance that had brought them here, and she asked about mine. She was here to take care of Madison, whose parents couldn't bear to leave her home in Iowa. Their newborn baby girl's kidneys had been failing. The doctor in Iowa said there wasn't any way for them to help her there and suggested taking her off life support. "My son and his wife are young parents, just twenty years old; it was just too hard for them.

They couldn't bring themselves to do it, so, instead, they just waited for something to happen."

She shared how congenital kidney disease had affected her family: family members born with just one kidney or, tragically, none at all. "Last year I lost a grandson who was born without kidneys. He lived only hours. My daughter's doctor encouraged her to end her pregnancy, but she refused. She knew she would lose her child, but she carried him to delivery anyway. She cherished the few hours she had with him," she said. "We have a large family. Many people were praying for Madison's sister when her kidneys started to fail. Three days after the doctors told them there was no hope, they started to function a bit, enough that it wasn't hopeless any longer."

The baby had been airlifted by helicopter, while the rest of them drove the five-hour trip from Iowa to Minneapolis. Upon the baby's arrival at Children's, they determined there might be a surgical option to help her. "Surgery was yesterday, and it looks like it worked. Now we have to just wait and see." Then, "There they are now," she said, smiling as she gazed through the glass that lined a wall of the waiting room. I looked up to see Madison's mom and dad walking on either side of a covered Isolette pushed by a nurse in pastel printed scrubs. Madison's dad noticed his mom as he looked through the glass. He smiled at her through his exhaustion, as if to say, "She's made it, Mom." There was unusual depth in his face, far beyond his young age.

Paul joined us in the waiting room. We sat and talked about Charlie and how much we missed Sophie. Madison found a spot nestled next to me on the sofa.

Paul reached for the waiting room phone to call and check on Sophie. He talked quietly with his mom in Arabic, leaving me ignorant of their conversation. Once he was finished, he handed me the phone so I could talk to Sophie. She didn't say hello. Instead, she asked, "Mommy, why can't Charlie open his eyes?" Her question knocked the wind from me. There I sat with someone else's toddler snuggled next to me, paralyzed. Tears instantly streamed down my face. Sophie rarely spoke in Arabic, but her comprehension was spot on. "Mommy? Mommy? When will he open his eyes, Mommy?" she asked in a bit of a panic. Paul looked at me intently, realizing I was on the edge of something. He shook his head as if to say, "Keep it together, honey. Please, for Sophie, keep it together."

I swallowed hard and mustered as much control as possible. Even so, my voice still came out in a quiver. I said, "He can't open his eyes yet, honey, because he is too sick."

Without a moment's pause, she asked, "When he gets better, then he'll open them, right, Mommy?"

"Right, honey," I replied. I told her I loved her, and I handed the phone back to Paul.

Madison was still by my side as I tried to catch my breath. I looked over to her grandmother, realizing that I didn't even know her name. It was quiet and intimate in the room. She didn't know my name either, and yet she chose to sit with me in my pain. It was then that I realized that

I hadn't seen my son's eyes. It hadn't occurred to me until that moment, and suddenly it was all I could think about. It was something else I would wait for: the color of my baby's eyes.

Talking to God

"Have you been home yet?" Karen asked from the other side of the Isolette. Karen, Charlie's nurse, was with us for most of the time we spent in the NICU. She even volunteered to work double shifts in order to be with Charlie. She knew cardiac care. She was confident and skilled, and had a less flowery, no-coddle approach. She was single, full-figured, and somewhere in her thirties. She had short, blonde, heavily styled hair that somehow suited her no-nonsense attitude. I became attached very quickly. I was thankful for her, less flower and all.

"Not yet," I replied, "but we talked about going home today to get some clean clothes and things."

"You need to prepare yourself the best you can for how difficult it will be to go home without your baby," she said. "Parents don't always anticipate the emotional impact of going home with empty arms." I heard her, but I was quick to dismiss it. *How much harder can this get?* Besides, we had known for months now that having to leave him at the hospital would be a real possibility.

A few hours later, Paul pushed open the heavy hospital door leading onto the top level of the parking ramp. We stepped out into the day, and I instinctively took a deep, cleansing breath of fresh air. I stood with my eyes closed and my face toward the sky, the cool spring breeze on my cheeks. I had gone days without stepping outside.

I heard it in the distance at first, the whooping, repetitive sound of a helicopter's propeller. It became louder and louder. I opened my eyes and, still gazing skyward, saw the halo effect of the circling propeller above us. The red emergency cross came into focus as the helicopter gently landed on the rooftop next to us. It was an impressive sight. Paul and I looked at one another with sadness. Somebody's baby was in that helicopter. Maybe their baby was fresh and new, or maybe their baby was fourteen years old. It was someone's baby all the same, and their lives were upside down too.

"It's not the first one I've seen land," Paul said to me. "I've seen them come and go a few times when I've been out here talking to God." "Talking to God" meant a little more than prayer for Paul. I don't mean to imply that he wasn't actually doing that—talking to God—because I am sure he was. It's just that if he went out to "talk to God," he did so with either a cigarette or a cheap cigar.

Paul had confessed to me how his nicotine relapse occurred. It was late in the evening on the day of Charlie's birth. The dust had just started to settle from the chaos of the day. With his nerves unhinged, Paul walked out the front doors of the hospital, cut across the traffic on Chicago Avenue, and walked into the convenience store kitty-corner to the hospital. He walked up to the cashier, who sat behind a heavy pane of bullet-proof glass. Without hesitation, he asked for a pack of Marlboro Reds and a lighter. It was his first pack of cigarettes in more than two years, an addiction he had worked tirelessly to overcome. He didn't even make it back across the street; instead, he sat on the curb, gas pumps behind him and city traffic in front of him, tapped his box of Reds on the cement, and lifted his first cigarette from the rest. He sat, he inhaled, and he talked to God.

Each mile we drove away from the hospital felt like twenty. I stared out the car window, watching the world move by. Our world had suddenly stopped, while the rest had the audacity to keep humming along. Half an hour later, we walked into the silence of our empty house. I sat on the staircase leading up to our bedrooms while Paul busied himself with our bags and mail.

I was attentive to a hollowness tucked deep inside me. It was the same place that had whispered for life when I knew I wanted my babies. Now there was emptiness, and it intensified with the absence of Sophie's footsteps. I was exhausted in a way I'd never experienced. The middle of my chest was heavy, as if something were pressing on my heart. The heaviness had come the moment Charlie was taken from me, and it had stayed with me ever since. Paul looked over to me from the stack of envelopes and said, "It's going to be okay. He's going to be okay." Then he set them down, came over, bent down, and held me. I sobbed, and I sobbed, and I sobbed. I told him that I knew he was right, Charlie *would* be okay. Still, I expressed how awful the pain was, how the suffering seemed unbearable, how I felt helpless in *his* suffering because, even though I was his *mom*, I couldn't make it better. I was broken too. I sobbed until my eyes ran dry and I'd flooded Paul's broad shoulders.

As Paul eased away from me, I continued to lie on the stairway. I pushed on, inviting Jesus to heal me, to give me strength. I asked him to embrace me in my brokenness. My body was limp and heavy with exhaustion, just like a sleeping child who is scooped up into her father's arms. I recognized his presence, not by his scent or the softness of his shirt collar. I recognized him by the calm that blanketed me. My eyes opened and closed drowsily until, finally, I surrendered to the fatigue. This is the part where, as a child, I would let my head drape heavily over his shoulder. There was magic here. He was strong and steady under me. His strength moved us. I was just along for the ride. It was the safest place in the world, the embrace of my *Father.* He took me up, readily and gladly.

I gathered myself from the staircase and moved forward. I washed clothes, gathered some things, and avoided the stillness of my babies' bedrooms. Then we hurried back to the hospital, where everything was just as it had been upon our departure. I sat at my son's bedside and asked Jesus to scoop him up, to embrace him in the same way he'd embraced me.

Fighting Dragons

*T*hey came unannounced, expressing that they just couldn't bear to stay away any longer. It was nice to have them there. We didn't know each other very well, but we had shared a powerful moment of prayer those weeks ago. Paul and I welcomed Larry and Susan's visit. We sat and chatted in a waiting room before bringing them back to meet Charlie. They had brought their teenage son with them, a young man of faith, because he too wanted to pray for our baby.

I told Susan that Charlie's doctors and nurses were impressed with his strength. He continued to progress with much stacked against him. Susan and Larry looked at each other, grinning, like they shared a secret.

She asked if we knew what Charlie's name meant. We knew that his middle name, Michael, meant "He Who Is Like God." We had chosen Charles as a first name early in our pregnancy, before we knew anything was wrong. We decided on his middle name after the heart diagnosis. I wanted Charlie to have a strong, intentional name—something with biblical significance. I loved the images of Michael the Archangel. "I wanted him to be as prepared as possible for whatever fight he was up against. Michael fights off a dragon. He's kind of a bad-ass," I said, feeling my lips turn up a bit at the corners.

"Why did you choose Charles?" Susan asked, smiling.

"If we were having a boy, Paul asked that he be named after his cousin, Charlie. Charlie had great character, and Paul valued that. It was important to him."

"Charles is Old English, and means 'Strong Man,'" she said. "Your son's name literally means 'Strong Man Who Is Like God.'"

Moving Mountains

The tears . . . streamed down, and I let them flow as freely as they would, making of them a pillow for my heart. On them it rested. —St. Augustine

O ne night, more than usual, I couldn't seem to walk away from Charlie's Isolette. The tears wouldn't stop. His night nurse had already settled well into her shift. The lights were dimmed, and the monitor sounds were softened. The clock inched toward midnight. His nurse had been gently nudging me toward the door for a good hour now. "We're here for him; he's getting all that he needs. You need to go home and get some rest," she said. Paul had gone to lie down in the Parent Sleep Room some time ago. I had convinced him that I would be leaving for home shortly.

The sleep room, that same one we'd been ushered into during the chaos of Charlie's first few hours, had become Paul's makeshift home. The room was held in reserve for parents whose babies were the most critical. Each morning parents were to turn in the key, and the staff would determine who would use the room that evening. For many days, Paul handed the key to a nurse each morning, and they handed it directly back to him. Eventually, they stopped accepting it and told us just to keep it indefinitely.

Paul developed a nightly ritual of standing at Charlie's Isolette and reciting prayers from a small Catholic prayer booklet he kept in his pocket. Eventually he would leave the NICU, surrendering to the nurse's request that he go and rest. Settling into the pullout sofa, he would give in to his exhaustion. He would sleep a couple of hours, but then fear would come without warning, jolting him from the sofa. Half asleep, he'd race back into the NICU to check on Charlie.

"I am having an especially hard time leaving him tonight," I expressed. I wanted to scoop Charlie up in my arms and nestle him into my chest. I wanted to feel his breath on my shoulders. "I haven't held him yet, you know, not even once," I said to his nurse, avoiding her glance and staring at Charlie's snugly closed eyes.

"I know you haven't," she said gently. "Hopefully, in the next couple of days he will be stable enough to hold. I know it must be very difficult for you, but I assure you he's getting the very best care. I think it would be best if you tried to go home and rest."

I pulled a little brown stuffed lion from my bag. It had a puffy, soft mane, a red nose made of thread, and a red ribbon around its neck. I nestled it into the Isolette. I leaned in and kissed the back of Charlie's head, breathing deeply to etch his smell into my memory. I picked up the other, identical brown lion that had been lying with him since that morning and put it carefully into my bag. These never-washed stuffed animals trapped his smell in a way my memory couldn't. It wasn't the typical baby smell of a newborn. Hospital staleness mingled with his baby scent, yet I still yearned for it. In his eight days of life, he hadn't had a bath—not even following his birth—because attempts at sponging him off sent his blood pressure soaring. My heart ached. I wanted to make myself tiny and lie close with him.

I sobbed all the way out of the building and into the parking ramp. The thought had crossed my mind that it was late and I should ask Security to walk me out to my car, but in my frazzled state, I hadn't thought it through. The ramp was sparsely populated as most cars at this late hour parked near the hospital entrances. As I walked further out into the ramp, I saw a couple walking toward me. I could see no car they had climbed out of. It was dark. The closer I got to my vehicle, the closer they came toward me. The hair at the base of my neck started to stand as I sensed danger.

She was young, but hardened beyond her years. Her heavily treated hair was wild, and her darkened eyes were sunken well into her emaciated frame. Her counterpart, a tall, broad man, walked swiftly with his hands tightly stuffed into his jean pockets. He wore a baseball cap, with a tattered sweatshirt hood pulled up over it, concealing parts of his face.

I continued to sob as I walked toward my car. My heart ached; my body ached. With each step, pain shot through my pelvis. I still hadn't given my body a chance to rest. I was also in desperate need of a breast pump, and pain ran through my right breast. I looked up and saw the couple still coming toward me. My eyes met hers, and I prayed, "Lord, help me." She saw my misery. I saw hers. She looked to him and turned her head slightly, as if to say "Not her." I reached my car, heart pounding, locked myself inside, lay my head against the cold steering wheel, and continued to cry.

My drive home was a distorted mess of city lights and sounds through my tear-soaked eyes. I listened to Gospel singer Ginny Owens' jazzy rendition of "If You Want Me To" over and over:

It may not be the way I would have chosen
When you lead me through a world that's not my home
But You never said it would be easy
You only said I'd never go alone
So when the whole world turns against me
And I'm all by myself
And I can't hear You answer my cries for help
I'll remember the suffering Your love put You through
And I will go through the valley if You want me to.

Finally home, I sat in the dark of my quiet kitchen and started the monotonous chore of expressing breast milk. I had rented a hospital-grade pump from the NICU. It was an impressive piece of equipment that made the little $300 pump in the sleek black leather bag look like child's play. This brute was intended for continual use, when Mom and Baby are separated for long periods of time. I heard discouragement from some of the nursing staff over my intention to breast-feed. They said things like "You know, preparing to nurse means you're going to need to set an alarm in the middle of the night, every couple of hours, to pump. It's a huge commitment during an already exhausting time," or something of the sort. Their tone was sweet and concerned—a bit too sweet. What I heard sounded more like "Seriously, don't you think you have enough on your plate? You have no idea what you're up against here, with a special-needs infant. Get some sleep now while you can. Your intention is good, but in the whole scheme of things, your breast milk isn't going to move mountains."

I appreciated their well-intended sentiment, but it was more than milk. I hadn't been able to comfort him. I hadn't changed a diaper, or maneuvered a baby-blue onesie over his head. I certainly hadn't performed any heroic medical intervention to keep him alive. Up until this moment, I had only stood by his Isolette, as helpless as he. My milk was something that only I could give to him, so I needed to.

Now, however, I knew something was wrong. My right breast was hot to the touch, and fiery red. The initial sequence of the pump made me cry out in pain. I looked down into the bottle, alarmed by the cloudy, greenish, blood-stained liquid dripping to the bottom. Mastitis.

I crawled into bed with a heating pad to my breast. I surrounded myself with every pillow in the house in an attempt to lessen my loneliness. I nestled Charlie's brave little lion into my makeshift cocoon. I thought about Sophie, and wondered what her day had been like. I missed her. I missed my husband. I imagined the color of Charlie's eyes, again. I let the tears gently roll from my face onto my pillow. I asked Jesus to hold me once more.

The LORD is close to the brokenhearted and saves those who are crushed in spirit. —Psalm 34:18 (New International Version)

Midnight Blue

*W*ith the darkness of that sorrowful night behind me, the next day brought with it a much needed moment of hope.

As I arrived at the hospital early the next morning, the night-shift nurses were at the end of their workday. I scrubbed my hands as quickly as I could at the sink in the doorway of Charlie's unit—the first of many scrub-downs that day, like every day. The smell of the disinfectant was familiar now, and it drew thoughts of Charlie. I made my way over to his Isolette, and his nurse smiled at me. She stepped away a bit as I asked her how his night had been and how he was doing now. She smiled wider and said, "Why don't you take a peek?"

I was brought to a place of such joy-I expressed myself like a wide-eyed child. "His eyes are open! He's awake!" I cried out. The sound of my voice sent his eyes searching for me. His ventilator kept him from turning his head, but his eyes searched nonetheless. I bent down toward Charlie's face, and for the first time our eyes met. "Oh, honey," I said, "I'm your mommy. It's so nice to meet you!" I was overcome with joy, and I hid none of it. "His eyes are blue! He's looking at me!" I cried out to the nurses without letting my eyes leave his. They were indeed midnight blue, the darkest, most beautiful, deepest blue I'd ever seen. "I've missed you so much, and I'm so glad you're finally here with me," I said to him, tears running down my face. His eyes were amazingly alert, as if he was trying to make sense of this place he was in. There was depth in his gaze, and I opened my heart to him more than ever before. I hoped he would see me. I looked up from his Isolette to see three nurses standing near, tissue box in hand. "Isn't he beautiful? He is so beautiful!" I said.

"Yes, he is," Charlie's nurse replied, her face wet with emotion. "I think he's been looking for you. He's been alert like this on and off through the night," she said, smiling.

Silent Cries

A NICU is often eerily quiet. There are babies lined up, one after the other, and yet there is no crying, at least not that anyone hears. They had reduced Charlie's sedation, allowing him to be awake more often. Amy was one of his night nurses. She was perky and petite with bobbed, dark brown hair. She had the energy of a wound-up teenage girl, although the lines in her face and her admission to having four of her own children, two of whom were well into their teens, put her somewhere in her forties. She was the kind of nurse who would spend time talking to your baby, even if no one was around to hear.

"It's so quiet in here—all of these babies, and there is no crying. I think I'd rather hear crying," I expressed to Amy.

"Oh, there is crying; you just can't hear it because of the ventilators. You can see it in their little bodies. It's hard to watch," she said.

Amy recognized our last name and was giddy to find out that Paul's uncle was her tennis instructor. In fact, Uncle Ab taught a group of Amy's co-workers as well. We chatted about things that had nothing to do with sick babies. She went on about what a great instructor Ab was, and how much they enjoyed their lessons. She was excited to take part in her first tennis tournament. She said they were thinking about what to wear to the tournament, and had asked Ab if they should order tennis skirts. She said he had told them they didn't play well enough to wear skirts. "Actually, what he said was, 'Tennis skirts are for people who have a chance in hell of winning; you, my dear, should stick to your exercise shorts.'" She giggled in a self-deprecating sort of way. "He says just what he means, and he's right, I really don't have any business wearing a tennis skirt," she said, and we laughed. It was nice to think of something outside these walls, even for just a moment.

Then, looking down at Charlie, she said, "Oh, buddy, don't cry, what is it you need?" My heart sank. You could indeed see it in every inch of him: the way his chest rose and fell, the way his lips quivered around the ventilator tube, and, most telling, the way his little face scrunched up tight.

There hadn't been a moment that I didn't want to scoop him up in my arms, but now I felt a mad, heart-wrenching level of wanting. I couldn't make it better for him, whatever it was, whatever he needed. I just stood at his side, stroked the top of his head, and talked gently to him. I hated my powerlessness in this. "I can't help him; there is nothing I can do to help him."

Amy came and stood with me. Tenderly she said, "He knows you're here with him; he knows your voice, and it comforts him." My tone was ugly with cynicism as I told her that I hoped she was right. She pointed to his blood pressure that had inched its way down again and said, "I can see it in his stats. He responds to the sound of your voice. Remember, your voice is the first voice he's ever known." I took a few minutes to sulk before acknowledging that at least it was something.

Holy Water

We discussed Charlie's baptism with our senior pastor, Jim, when he came to visit with us at the hospital. He is kind and soft-spoken. He wears a neatly groomed, full gray beard. His hair, also full, is salt-and-peppered, contrasting with the crystal blue of his eyes. He stood patiently next to Charlie and listened to my concerns.

We were certain that we wanted to have him baptized before his open-heart surgery. Yet, I was unsettled. I worried that our decision to have a hospital baptism would project things we didn't intend. I didn't believe that Charlie's salvation was dependent on baptism. I knew that Jesus held him now, and would hold him forever. We hadn't given up hope either; we were anticipating the very best for him. I didn't want anyone believing otherwise, and I certainly didn't want to give power to it. Still, I wanted this sacrament for him.

When I was finished with my anxious ramblings, Pastor Jim's response to me was simple. He said, "We believe that in infant baptism, God sends his Holy Spirit to miraculously place the gift of faith on a person's heart. Baptism is God's gift to each of us. Why shouldn't we bless him now with this gift?" God's whisper was within the silence that followed; what I heard was, *Let the rest fade away*.

We waited anxiously the following morning for another one of our pastors, Pastor Connie, to arrive. Pastor Jim had expressed that he thought Pastor Connie would be an exceptional blessing to us in this. I was afraid that his baptism would become a somber occasion, when what I wanted for Charlie was a celebration. Karen was his nurse that morning (the confident, less flowery one). We told her that one of our pastors was coming, and that we were having Charlie baptized today. She brought in some partitions to surround us. Although well-intended, it provided little privacy.

Pastor Connie came into the NICU wearing a vibrant, multicolored stole around her shoulders, matching the vibrancy in her presence. Pastor Connie is a beautiful woman. She's tall, with sleek, blonde, chin-length hair that frames her face. She has a wide pirate's smile that matches the radiance in her eyes. Her face is soft and touched with lines from living well.

She embraced us, and we settled in around Charlie's Isolette. She asked us how we were, and how Charlie was doing. I was taken aback that she didn't seem fazed by the abundance of equipment and IVs. Then she began to share. She told us that her son had been born with a form of dwarfism and had to endure countless surgeries and interventions. She said that the day she realized her son belonged to Jesus, not her, was the day she began to move forward in Jesus' light. She learned to go to him in petition for all things. She and her husband prayed endlessly for their son's growth and development. Before each surgery, she would ask Jesus to hold him. Smiling, she said, "David grew to be five feet, five inches tall, which is extraordinarily tall for his type of dwarfism. His doctors simply have no answers for his height. He is living a full life now. He is a talented musician. He's met a delightful girl, and they are talking about marriage."

We prayed for Charlie, and then Pastor Connie began the Sacrament of Holy Baptism for him. Her tone and presence lifted even more. It was as if she were unaware of our surroundings, as if she stood in front of a congregation on a bright Sunday morning. The partitions that surrounded us seemed silly now, as Pastor Connie's joyfulness couldn't be contained. It lifted up and over the makeshift walls, filling the whole room with her spirit. She delighted in Charlie just as he was, calling him a child of God. She made no reference to his ill health; instead she rejoiced in God's gifts to him. She poured holy water over the top of his head, baptizing him "in the name of the Father, and of the Son, and of the Holy Spirit."

I looked up from Charlie to see his nurse, Karen. Her face was filled with a softness I hadn't seen before. She stood at a distance, yet she was fully engaged. Her attempt to contain her emotion was to no avail. As she stepped in closer to us to silence a monitor, she wiped tears from her face. Pastor Connie offered us no sympathy, only joy. She delighted in what we had been given on this day.

Her presence was refreshing and hopeful, and God's spirit shone through her.

A Letter to Charles

April 27, 2005

*M*y sweet little boy,
You are nine days old today. Each of these days since your birth, a thousand times, I've wanted nothing more than to scoop you up into my arms and nestle your warm little body into mine. Each time I've seen your pain, I've wanted to detach you from all the ways you've been tied down. I've wanted to lift you up onto my shoulder, and we would pace the room together, with your breath on my neck. There would be a gentle bounce in my step, while I whisper in your ear, shushing away all your hurts. If only.

Today Karen placed you in my arms, and Daddy got his turn too. We were nervous; how silly. Yesterday, after my persistent asking, Karen assured me that we would get to hold you before surgery, no matter how unstable you were. "Parents ALWAYS hold before surgery," she said. I know her bold tone was for my assurance, but it only led me to ponder why parents ALWAYS held their babies before surgery.

It actually took two nurses to place you on my lap. Because Karen is such a smart lady, and you are such a special boy, there has been a student nurse at Karen's side. She watches you intensely. She's young and naturally pretty. She stood by at your baptism. Her eyes are doe-like; she wears no make-up and has thick wavy hair that naturally stays back and away from her face. She says very little; mostly she stands and waits for Karen's direction. Watching her expressions, I see you have a little piece of her heart. She helped Karen move you from your Isolette and into our arms. It was no easy task.

I rocked you back and forth, soothing the rawness of my heart. Daddy leaned into us as close as he could. We admired the way you held your fists up close to your chubby cheeks. We marveled at how much you resemble your sister. Your attributes are so similar to hers, only yours are masculine. Daddy and I enjoyed our time with you very much. Nonetheless, I still felt unsatisfied.

You weren't close enough for me. Instead of nestling in, you were placed on top of a pillow that lay on top of me. All the things that were attached to you—I had to hold onto them too. I closed my eyes and felt your weight in my arms. I imagined the equipment fading away.

And so I will wait, Charlie. I will wait for you. We will surely have our time. When the rest of the world is tucked in at night, you and I will sit and rock. We will have our time when no one is watching. I will open the blinds in the big window of your room, and we will look out into the dark summer night together. I will hush away your hurts, and there will be nothing that ties you down.

XOXO,

Mommy

Crossing Bridges

*D*espite ugly circumstances, sometimes moving forward seems too big of a bridge to cross. Sometimes it feels easier to just settle in the ugly.

I was horribly uncomfortable the last few weeks of my pregnancy with Sophie. I woke up multiple times each night needing to use the bathroom. Paul said there was a great deal of annoying grunting and heavy breathing as I worked at hoisting myself from bed. Lucky for him, he was smart enough to keep this annoyance to himself (that is, until months afterward, when he felt it was safe to share). Finally, after waddling to the bathroom, I would empty four whole drops of pee from my flattened bladder. I gained forty pounds during the pregnancy, most of which spanned the short distance from my ribcage to my pelvis, all within my petite 5-foot, 2-inch frame. I was a caricature of a pregnant housewife, like one of those satirical pencil sketches from the '60s. I even wore what looked like a muumuu dress, a long, floral nightgown that had a "sexy" tent look to it.

I had terrible sciatic pain which forced me to waddle sideways, dragging my right leg along with a two-second delay. Witnessing my strange gait as I left an OB check, my doctor decided enough was enough. It was time to yell "uncle." My induction was scheduled for the following morning.

So one might think I would be geared up to get this over with, right? That it was time to regain ownership of my increasingly crippled body? Well, that would seem logical. But I lay in bed that evening, and in between the hoisting and the grunting, I convinced myself that this wasn't so bad after all. I could stay this way indefinitely; sure, it would be incredibly uncomfortable, not to mention probably physically impossible, but at least I *knew this* uncomfortable place. Better the pain you know than the uncertainty you fear. I wanted to see Miss Sophie's face like nothing else, but there was this one thing that stood between us.

Childbirth. Wowza.

After a couple of hours of lying there planning my pregnancy extension, reason started to creep in. Much to my delusional dismay, I recognized I had no choice in this. This childbirth thing was probably inevitable. I sulked like a spoiled child.

The next morning I was full of nerves and fear. Sure, there was excitement too, but it was overshadowed by the ugly stuff. My labor nurse started me on Pitocin, and every few minutes I had a contraction. Much to my surprise, I was handling things quite well and felt good about my "progress," thank you. My nurse, however, was not impressed. She decided that breaking my water might just help to "move things along."

It took a whole ten minutes for the pain to start rolling in, but then my contractions came one on top of the other. What was happening to me? I was supposed to have a break in between contractions. I had learned that in our birthing class (gee, *that* wasn't a ridiculous waste of time at all). Nope, mine just kept on a-comin'. Not to be overly dramatic, but seriously, I wondered if I might never come out on the other end of the continual pain. I hadn't planned on an epidural; I thought they were creepy. It wasn't part of my stupid birth plan either. But I hadn't anticipated this level of pain; who knew this was even possible? So I managed to get the words out: "I need an epidural." As I remember it, the only other words I uttered during labor were "Something's wrong; why aren't there any breaks?"

My nurse's fancy-pants reply to my request? "Honey, we aren't going to have an epidural; we are about to have a baby."

In other words, it was too late for an epidural. I had no choice but to make my way through. This was really happening, that was for sure. Whether or not I was ready was insignificant.

Sophie was born two and a half hours after that first hard contraction. I didn't just cross the bridge; I catapulted to the other side. The moment she was born and the doctor laid her on my chest, all of that intense pain that had overwhelmed me melted away.

At that time in my life, braving childbirth was the biggest challenge I'd ever faced. Left to my own devices, I might have chosen to use my body as a permanent hotel and found some muumuus that complemented my eyes. But life continues to move forward even amid our reluctance. In the end, all my pain and discomfort seemed insignificant. It was worth it a million times over. I started that day as a fearful young woman, and ended in a place of gratitude I had never known. I held a precious, tiny little person in my arms. She smelled fresh from heaven, and she would grow to call me Mommy.

Now, here we were, three years later, and I faced this new challenge with the same irrational reluctance. Charlie was inching his way toward his open-heart surgery. Each day he got closer and closer to having lost enough excess fluid to clear him for surgery. He would be graduating from the NICU into the PICU (Pediatric Intensive Care Unit), where he would stay a day or two before surgery and where he would recover during the bumpy days to follow.

This was a whole new unit of a whole new floor in the hospital. Dr. Singh would still be with us, but there would be new doctors and nurses, none of whom knew our baby's name. They didn't know his sister's name either, or the fact that my husband, despite his hard appearance, prefers coddling. They didn't know that on a bad day I don't have an emotional filter and I say just what I feel, even if it should be an "inside thought."

We had just settled into a routine in the NICU; we knew what our days looked like there. The staff there had orchestrated the frenzy around his birth. They had helped save him, and as the dust settled around him, they painstakingly attended to his every need. Now we were going to be dropped on another floor to begin again?

My irrational thought: Why couldn't we just stay in the NICU indefinitely? Sure, things were painfully uncomfortable, but this was our new normal, and I'd already navigated through this. I was scared of what lay around the corner. If

I allowed us to move forward, it would bring ever closer the day I'd have to hand my son over to an operating room team, the day when I'd have to pray that the next time I touched his soft little cheek, it would still be warm with life. Just as I had tried to do the night before Sophie was born, I wanted to stop this from happening. For a short while I deluded myself into believing I had that control.

Paul had spent the evening prior with Sophie at his parents' house. I hurried at home alone that morning, hoping not to miss Charlie's departure from the NICU. Upon my arrival, I saw that Karen was not with him. I decided that was probably for the best; I was more attached to her than any of the others. Today's nurse was less familiar, though still a face I recognized as one of the many who had helped in his first few hours. As she prepared him for his move, she marveled at his progress since that first chaotic day. She made all of his monitors and IVs mobile by tucking in and winding up the miles of cords. She gathered all of his things. When she carefully took down his picture of the sweet, chubby teddy bear with his name across the top, it struck a rawness in me and I screamed on the inside, *No, no, he's not ready! We're not ready for this! This bridge is too big; I want to stay here on this side!* But she continued on, taking great care so as not to damage it. With everything set to move, she called down to his new room to ensure that they were ready for him.

With another nurse there to help, we started our little journey. Charlie's heart rate and blood pressure monitor were the last cords to be pulled from the wall. This intensified my anxiety. How would we know if he suddenly started to spiral while en route and unplugged? They slowly moved his Isolette out of its spot. We started moving toward the door. I turned to see the emptiness where we had been. Watching me as intently as the mess of equipment, the nurse said, "I know this can be hard, but I can assure you he'll get the same great care downstairs." She must have heard my screams.

Paul and I had toured the PICU with one of their nurses the day before. She buzzed us through the secure unit and it felt like we were entering an entirely new hospital. It was darker, the lights were dimmed, and the walls were a darkened yellow tone. We were centered deep within the hospital, so there were no windows to let in outside light. Our presence was met with polite smiles, as though we'd been invited into something privileged.

The unit was essentially square, with private and semi-private rooms lining its perimeter. Along one of the four sides was the "bay," a series of beds lined up facing the nurses' main station. In contrast to other areas of the unit, there was little privacy in the bay. Curtains could be pulled to surround each bed, but most were left open. The openness, we were told, allowed for multiple eyes and ears on critical patients at all times. It was likely the area where Charlie would stay, at least initially. There were no Isolettes here; even the tiniest of babies was laid upon a full-sized hospital bed.

We stopped to see another cardiac baby recovering from surgery. It felt crushing to walk in on someone else's misery. He was tiny, and his skin had the oddest yellow tone. His chest was concave. Drainage tubes filled with blood came from the bottom of his chest and ran all the way down the length of the bed, emptying into a reservoir at the foot. We were told that his parents had stepped away for dinner. "This little guy is having a difficult time. Recovery looks different for each baby, but I wanted you to have an idea of what to expect," the nurse said.

I was anxious. Though this baby was not mine, my instinct was to cover his little body, shielding him from the eyes of people walking by. "I can't believe he is so exposed, just right out in the open for everybody to see," I said. She responded by reminding us that the unit was secure, and visitors were told of the importance of patient privacy.

"I had to get permission from his parents to allow you to see him," she said. Still, we were only two steps from an open hallway. His privacy curtain was wide open. I knew her statement was well intended, but it was silly.

The image of him remained etched in my mind's eye, even as we made our way into the unit with Charlie the following day. I couldn't help but think of this other child, broken and exposed.

I walked next to Charlie's moving Isolette as his nurse explained that since the introduction of the HIPPA privacy law, once a baby leaves their unit, they are no longer privileged to that patient's information. "I know this transition is hard for parents, but believe me, it's difficult for us too." Smiling, she said, "Please remember us. We would love to know how Charlie is doing in his recovery."

Much to my surprise, she pulled Charlie into one of the private rooms, where a couple of nurses started helping to get him situated. "I thought he was supposed to be in the bay?" I questioned.

"Well, he may or may not end up there, but the bay is full right now," one of the PICU nurses said callously, as if we were trying to unload a case of expired fruit at the market. I was already annoyed. Her name was Danny, and she was frosty. She looked Charlie over, pointed to the IV that came out of his head, and said, "Well *that* will be changed out." The disdain in her tone was sharp, and she spoke to no one in particular.

Our NICU nurse turned to say her goodbyes. She reminded us to check in, and that they would all be thinking of Charlie. I watched her turn and leave, feeling like an anxious child who had been dropped at a daycare center.

Danny explained that Charlie's new doctor, an intensivist, would likely be in shortly to take a look at him. "He will want to change out some IVs, especially the one in his head. He will also insert an arterial line." She explained that an arterial line is placed deep, directly into an artery, and monitors blood pressure more accurately. It also would allow for them to get arterial blood gas measurements. My stomach started to turn.

Soon, the intensivist came in and introduced himself. He was tall and thin and had a studious appearance. He explained that it was their goal to ensure that children were always as comfortable as possible. Charlie would be heavily sedated as he placed the arterial line and possibly changed out some other IVs. He asked me to leave, explaining that parents are not usually present during placement.

I reluctantly walked away, praying that Jesus would stay. I needed a moment anyway to call Paul and vent about our new frosty nurse. I found my way out of the unit, walking past the baby boy whose image had been etched into my mind. He looked just as he had the day before, only now his mama was at his side. She sat leaning up against his bed, her arms extended close to his tiny body.

The bridge was crossed, and my heart was heavy.

Circus Murals

She was only two doors down from us, rendering it impossible not to notice the stream of activity in and out of her room. Somber faces came and went, ushered in, two at a time. Her cardiologist was the same one who performed Charlie's septostomy that first day; I recognized him as he met with her family at her bedside. I watched him from a distance as he talked with them. I thought about how he'd seen the inside of Charlie's heart. I wondered how different her heart was from my son's. The lights were always dimmed in her room, and she was never awake.

The table next to her bed had framed pictures of her loved ones, along with a colorful bouquet of spring flowers. I wondered how much she heard of their whispers as they stood at her side. On the wall next to her bed was a mural of circus animals being pulled in a wagon. She was covered in a brightly colored handmade quilt. The curious part, even though she was tucked inside this Pediatric Intensive Care Unit, was that she wasn't a child at all. She looked easily forty or so.

She was part of the first generation of congenital heart defect survivors. The cardiac doctors at the renowned heart hospital next door—the ones who roto-rooter the fried-chicken fat from the arteries of older adults—wouldn't recognize this woman's heart. The doctor standing at her side—the one who knew that carving a hole deep inside my son's heart would temporarily keep him alive—*he* knew her heart. So it was here that she came to rest, lying with the circus mural off to her side.

The "private" rooms here had a full glass wall on one side, making it impossible not to see another patient's circumstance. Each time we walked past, we could see her loved ones absorbed in their vigil. I thought about her life as a child, wondering what it had looked like.

I hadn't considered how Charlie's life would look in adulthood. It was hard to imagine him at forty. It was enough to be consumed with getting him untied and pinked up, and bringing him home to his nursery. My mind dabbled in the realm of adulthood for a bit, thinking about life expectancy outside these walls, but I did my best to stay grounded. One day at a time. *Jesus, please, just one day at a time.*

Each room here had a story. In the room to the other side of us lay a toddler with a blood disorder. Her room was filled with huge Dora the Explorer balloons. One was shaped as the number two, as she spent her second birthday here in Intensive Care. She was on her third hospital visit of the year. Sitting next to Charlie, I heard her crying. I closed my eyes and tried to imagine her running and playing outside. I saw her giggling, skipping along, the sun glistening off her fresh cocoa skin and her dark locks wild in the wind.

Wrapped in our own story, Paul and I sat next to each other on one side of Charlie's bed, while Danny, the PICU nurse who had first gotten us settled in, sat on the other. She had mentioned to me as we settled in that each new heart family gets her "marriage talk." Since Paul was here now, I presumed she saw this as her opportunity. I was partly annoyed and partly intrigued. I was certain we weren't here for marriage counseling, but I sat and listened, knowing that I had nowhere else to go.

Danny started by sharing how she had cared for a little girl who needed multiple hospitalizations over the course of six years. The little girl's mom stayed close to her daughter's bedside during each one, while her husband spent his time watching sporting events on whatever waiting room television he could find. His detachment upset his wife terribly. Their daughter eventually lost her battle and died at six years of age. The couple's marriage was left in shambles; they divorced shortly after her death.

She expressed how everyone deals with the stress of such illness differently, and just because he wasn't at the bedside didn't mean that he didn't love his daughter. She went on to say that we should be respectful as to how each of us might cope differently. Danny thought the man's wife should have been more understanding.

Her counseling intervention, however well-intended, lacked boundaries. I was annoyed. She didn't know how it felt to watch her own child suffer. There was a difference between caring for families in crisis and being *in* the crisis. She couldn't know what it was like to have your husband detach emotionally, leaving you with the burden. Besides, how could she know the complexities of their marriage? Her little talk was self-serving, a way for her to express all that she had witnessed in her career. Wasn't she so smart and special?

Her words didn't give me any insight in protecting my marriage. Instead, she left me upset and worried. Not about the state of my marriage; rather, now I worried about the length of my crisis. I felt myself swirling in empathy for this nameless family's loss. The pain of losing their six-year-old must have been unbearable.

I needed to step away from this for a moment. I needed some time with Paul so I could unload the heaviness of this conversation. I didn't like leaving Charlie with her. It wasn't that I thought she lacked skills; she lacked *warmth*. She came off as cool and flippant. She could use a "talk" of her own, but I didn't have the energy. I guess I too needed coddling every now and again, and Danny was no coddler.

Paul and I headed down the hallway and through a waiting area that led us out of the secure unit. As we passed through, I caught the eye of another cardiac mom I'd noticed in the waiting area before. We smiled empathetically at one another. In her thick Russian accent, she asked how our son was. I asked about hers. I was grateful for the language barrier that only allowed for simple responses. I quickly excused myself, feeling overburdened.

We walked through the increasingly familiar corridors making our way to the basement cafeteria. Paul reached out for my hand. He looked broken and scared. He interrupted our silent walk with, "Six years of being in and out of here, multiple surgeries, all of that—and then she dies?" Apparently I wasn't the only one who had missed the mark of Danny's supposed marriage intervention.

"That wasn't okay. She doesn't know us—and she probably didn't really know them either," I said. "I would hate you for abandoning me at a hospital bedside." He gripped my hand tighter and gave me a sideways sarcastic glance, like *Come on, really?* "I know you wouldn't leave us," I said. "I'm just saying, how could she defend a father like that?"

Paul, who is often far less critical than I, said, "Give her a break. I'm sure she meant well." His thoughts were still elsewhere. "Six years . . . six *years* in this place." He shook his head as the words came from his lips. "I couldn't deal with it—with losing a six-year-old child—no way! I think I would go crazy from the pain."

Yes, six years was unthinkable. Already, I couldn't separate my pain from the pain of another. I felt like I was managing these burdens like a circus artist. Each new experience, each new family, each new heartache we encountered added to the last; I was like a circus performer spinning fiery rings on my every appendage. Fragile, exhausted, and unsettled, I waited for everything to come crashing to the floor, ending in a mess of shared broken sorrow. It was paralyzing.

The Arrival of Francis Moga

He didn't so much walk in; it was more like an easy shuffle, his feet never fully leaving the ground—the same way you would walk around your house in fuzzy slippers. He wore surgical scrubs and an unassuming, boy-like smile. Danny had mentioned earlier that Dr. Moga, Charlie's surgeon, would probably stop by to introduce himself, but I was taken aback when she greeted him with a casual "Hi, Frank." She turned to us, smiling, and said, "This is Dr. Moga." I wasn't sure what I had expected him to look like. Nonetheless, he didn't fit the image I had subconsciously conjured up.

Dr. Moga was tall, with a slender, athletic build. His smile was soft and shy. With his hairline starting to recede slightly, and with just a hint of age around his eyes, I decided he was either forty or quickly approaching it. He was charming in the most modest way.

After our introductions, he spent a moment looking at Charlie. I watched him intently, imagining my son's life cradled in his hands. I recalled, having read it somewhere along the way, that there were only seventy Pediatric Heart Surgeons in the country—only seventy. There was something strangely familiar about him, like we'd known each other somehow, somewhere. It's something I've never put to rest to this day.

Dr. Moga reviewed Charlie's chart, noted the amount of excess fluid Charlie had lost since his septostomy, among other factors, and said, "Well, I think we're ready to look at scheduling surgery. How does Friday sound?" Paul and I looked at each other, nervous and childlike, as if we'd just been called on amid a full classroom of students. I was speechless. Friday was only three days away and, as "luck" would have it, happened to be Paul's birthday. *Of all the days this could fall on, it falls on my husband's birthday?* One way or another, it would certainly change the significance of the day for the rest of Paul's life. With my tummy wrenched with nerves, I responded weakly with a meek "okay."

I asked about Dr. Singh and if he would be in the OR as well. "Absolutely," Dr. Moga replied. "Dr. Singh will be there, as will Dr. Overman. You haven't had the opportunity to meet my colleague Dr. Overman. He's been on vacation, but he'll be taking an early flight home." I looked at him questioningly. He answered me by saying, "There is this special little boy here with Transposition who is ready for surgery."

A New Day at the Circus

The following morning I walked by the woman's room, the one with the circus mural, to find it dark and empty. She was gone, as were the pretty flowers and handmade quilt. She must have passed away during the night. This experience in the ICU was so emotionally taxing.

I walked in to Charlie's room to find an unfamiliar nurse at his bedside. She looked up at me, smiling warmly. She told me her name was Paula. She must have been sixty or so. She had jet-black hair and porcelain-white skin. I asked her how Charlie was. Her response about his stats was lightning-fast as if she had more important things to talk about. She sighed and said, "Oh, I am going to try my best to stay away from those cheeks of his, but it's not going to be easy! I mean, look at those *cheeks!* Have you *ever?!*" She was very kind, and I wanted to bottle her up in case I needed some of her later.

We chatted, just the two of us as time inched by. Paula was single; she had never married. She had no children of her own. She had worked at Children's for decades. I sat back and watched her, thinking about her career. She talked and sang to Charlie, as if it were just the two of them. *She's doing just what she was made to do,* I thought. It seemed the perfect fit. More than one nurse walked by, asking Paula if she'd managed to keep her lips off this one. I stepped out to meet my girl and husband for lunch, this time with confidence, knowing Charlie was truly being held.

Our time spent away from Charlie's bedside by no means removed us from our reality. Sometimes we sat in a waiting room staring blankly at a TV screen. We roamed the hallways. We saw children frail and bald, colorless and puffy, pulled by nurses or family members in red wagons. Oncology had its own secure floor which we never entered, but there were always "escapees" scattered around other floors. With their hospital stays often lengthy, it was no wonder they sought a bit of freedom.

Paul spent one evening chatting with the mother of an oncology patient. They had met in the Family Resource Center, an area tucked away from patient care. It looked like a small public library. There were shelves of donated books and magazines and a quiet reading area. There were also a half dozen or so computers. It was prior to smartphones and widespread wireless internet connections. Parents used the desktop computers to update their children's CaringBridge sites.

Paul sat down next to her at a computer, and they simultaneously updated the news about their broken worlds. She leaned toward him, her long braid falling into his space first, and asked what floor he was on. "This one; my son is in Intensive Care," he responded. He continued to share with her, explaining that we were preparing for open-heart surgery. She listened intently, careful not to miss the details.

"What about you?" he asked. She told him that her six-year-old daughter was in isolation on the Oncology floor. She had been diagnosed with cancer when she was two years old. This was the latest of many long hospital stays.

"She won't survive, so we are managing what time we have left with her," she expressed from a place of quiet acceptance. "She's my baby. I have three older, healthy children who need me too, but I can't leave my baby here, not even for a moment. So I manage the best I can, and I hope that my other children are getting by." She told Paul that she stayed with her daughter around the clock, sleeping in a chair next to her bed. "She's scared, and I don't ever want her to ask for me, and I'm not there."

When Paul shared his experience with me, he was visibly shaken, but grateful at the same time. His intimate conversation with a stranger had given him new perspective. We were now on the other side of "Oh, just as long as my children are healthy, that's the only thing that matters." For us, having an ill child was no longer tucked away in an inconceivable, horrid place. We were *there*. You might imagine it as desolate and lonely, but it isn't. We were one family of many, some of whom faced challenges so enormous they made ours look like an afternoon trip to urgent care. Here we all stood, inside the unthinkable, our shoulders brushing against one another, and we were still breathing.

Not only were we breathing, but we were learning to do so in a whole new way. I was aware of all that surrounded me. I soaked it all in, all of it—not just the good stuff. I was in the darkest time of my life. Yet, I found exceptional value in my experiences. All of this emerged as I became aware of the fragility in the breath of my children, and I was transformed.

One time as we returned to Charlie's room, at first we just stood in the doorway and watched from a distance. Paula, with her soft, well-aged hands nestled under Charlie, cradled him gently just a tiny bit off the bed. Her lips brushed against his cheeks as she sang and cooed to him. He was alert and smiling back at her.

There is a wall plaque that hangs in my kitchen that reads: "Life isn't about waiting for the storm to pass; it's about learning to dance in the rain." Paula and Charlie were in the middle of a storm, he in Intensive Care, multiple IVs running from him. Yet, they had chosen to dance. I was blessed by their light. I know Paul saw it too; it was undeniable.

Shawshank with Mr. Bean

Making the decision to have a child is momentous. It is to decide forever to have your heart go walking around outside your body. —Elizabeth Stone

The pressure was unending, ever since the day we brought Sophie in piggy tails to see a fuzzy picture of "her" baby. My anxiety took on true physical weightiness. It lay over my heart, pinning it down. The amount of pressure varied depending on how far I allowed my worry to take me. Tomorrow Charlie was scheduled for open-heart surgery. The pressure was as great as it had ever been, teetering on unbearable.

I sat in a chair at the end of his bed. From a distance, I tried to etch the shape of his face into my memory, just in case. The clock rapidly advanced with no regard for my pleas. Tonight, Paul and I would both stay at the hospital. We eventually gave in to the nurse's insistence that we rest. I put my lips to Charlie's cheek and inhaled deeply, attempting to take some of him with me. With the heaviness upon my heart tenfold, I reluctantly walked away.

We found our way into the PICU parent sleep area. It was an odd little maze tucked behind an adjacent doorway. The rooms were curiously shaped, undoubtedly having been wedged into a sliver of unused hospital space. The walls were cement cinder block from floor to ceiling, and the floor was covered with old hospital tiles. There were three sleep rooms, two of which opened into a common bathroom. It was dreary in a Shawshank sort of way.

This gypsy lifestyle was becoming familiar, I thought, as we settled in with only a handful of our things. Our room had two tiny loveseats, of sorts, up against opposite walls. Thin mattresses pulled out to balance on flimsy metal stands. The mattresses had been turned down with clean bedding. I wandered into the common bathroom, from which I could see directly into the adjacent room. Nobody was there, but personal items were lying around the space. I quickly shut the door, feeling that I'd invaded someone's privacy.

Back in our room, I felt uneasy and claustrophobic, wedged into this cold, odd space with another couple in the midst of their own crisis. Being there was ridiculously surreal, like I'd walked into my own black-and-white Alfred Hitchcock film. I unraveled the cord to my breast pump and found a place to plug it in. I sat motionless at an empty desk against the wall. Listening to the rhythmic *swoosh* of the pump, I allowed my exhaustion to seep into my core. A twinge of pain moved through my left side now, opposite of the mastitis. I paid little attention, letting it simply fade within my darkness.

"Mindy, honey, ah, are you looking at this? This should be interesting," Paul said to me as he sized up his mattress and its little metal frame. My Pauly, you see, doesn't quite reach that coveted six-foot mark; he's stout and stocky, with broad shoulders. He's the guy you wish you hadn't cut off in traffic once you get a peek at him. I watched him carefully inch his way onto it, as if attempting to crawl across a suspended ceiling. He managed to lie down carefully, and I heard him sigh with relief.

Only a moment passed before the middle of the mattress started sagging toward the floor. The frame started to fold into itself—my big teddy bear of a husband still inside. Suddenly, he was sandwiched inside, his feet above his head. As his ride came to an end, I heard from across our little room: "Uh, little help now, little help?"

His pleas for help were in vain as I was hooked to my breast pump. And besides, the sight of him sandwiched inside was so hysterical that I was useless anyhow. Watching him try to free himself was just as rewarding. He tried to flatten down the mattress by flailing his legs about. I swore I heard an instrumental soundtrack and a laughing British audience. It looked like a beefy Mr. Bean had gotten himself into another predicament. We were both laughing; it was just the kind of moment we needed.

I pulled out my mattress and, thankfully, it stayed put. Paul decided the floor was his safest bet, pulled his mattress off its frame, and laid it on the tiles at my feet. It was paper-thin. He admitted it was worthless and that he might just as well lie directly on the floor.

So there we were, nestled deep inside the hospital, the silence and the darkness overwhelming. Our only light came from a slit at the base of the bathroom door. Across the room, the red numbers of an alarm clock were suspended in the blackness. It was well past midnight. I sat up and looked down at Paul as the light from the bathroom filtered around him. "Happy birthday, honey," I said, even as the pressure on my chest ground increasingly inward. I lay back down and tried to calm myself. We prayed together, Paul and I, in the dark, his voice coming from below my feet.

I reminded myself of all the ways God had held me during this ordeal, and of all the ways he had shown himself to me. I ran my fingers over the inscription circling my wrist: "With God all things are possible. Matthew 19:26."

I lay awake with the discussion we had had with Dr. Moga earlier that evening running through my mind. We had talked about the challenge of Charlie's single coronary artery, and how it complicated his surgery. "I'll be thinking of Charlie tonight, that's for sure, and he'll be the first thing I think about in the morning," Dr. Moga had said to me with a warm smile. I wondered if he was sleeping now, or if he too lay awake.

I asked how many times Dr. Moga had seen a single coronary artery like Charlie's. His response to me . . . once, he thought; only one other time that he could remember, in the last ten years. There was no sugar-coating here. His honesty was brutal. He explained that switching Charlie's aorta artery and pulmonary artery was pretty straightforward. It was the movement of this single coronary artery that could get messy. There was no room for error, and if things didn't go smoothly, he wouldn't come off the heart-and-lung machine. He said he'd been on the phone with his mentor in Ohio, and they'd been walking through scenarios.

The conversation haunted me, so I turned to prayer. I felt Jesus there in the darkness. He wedged himself between the rawness of my heart and all that weighed down on me. The pain remained, yes, but I was no longer alone in it. I felt my pain melt into his, and we mourned together.

The morning came quickly. I had no power against time—no way to pause it. The handful of hours came and went, taunting me and pushing us closer and closer to surgery. We walked into Charlie's room and found Paul's eldest brother, Pierre, already at his bedside. It wasn't even seven o'clock and Pierre was dressed in a full suit and tie. Charlie was in the middle of a photo shoot. I smiled at his nurse, and she said, "Look, Charlie's entertaining; we're having a party in here." The flash was relentless as Pierre paced at the end of the bed, capturing Charlie's image in rapid fire.

A handmade booklet lay next to Charlie. A thoughtful midnight nursing arts-and-crafts project, it was made of yellow construction paper tied together with thin yellow ribbon. The cover was handwritten and read "Happy Birthday, Dad." The pages were decorated with a hodgepodge of kiddy stickers and photos of Charlie, taken by a nurse in the night. In one, his little mouth was wet with bubbles of saliva spilling around his ventilator. "Blowing Birthday Kisses" was written at the bottom. The last page had a sticker of Simba from *The Lion King,* and it read, "From your super-human little cub. Have a roaring good day! I will too."

Pierre was wound with nervous energy. I wondered if he had slept at all. He tried to mask his anxiety with a forced smile and frantic chatter. I saw right through it, as if he were made of glass and his pain in Technicolor. He had come nearly every day to see Charlie. A man who prefers to set his own sun, you could read the anxiety scribbled across his face. *Why did this happen? Why can't I make it stop?* Charlie had turned our tidy little world inside out.

I wasn't certain when they would take Charlie away, pushing him beyond some mechanical door where parents and their unhinged emotions weren't allowed. I needed quiet time alone with him. I needed to whisper softly to him, to tell him how much I adored him. I asked Pierre to leave us alone for a bit, hoping I wasn't offending him. "I was just about to leave. I've got to get to work anyway," he said. He bent down and kissed Charlie, then turned and swiftly walked away.

We managed to steal just a moment alone with Charlie before the room became a buzz of activity. I stood beside him, paralyzed with emotion. His anesthesiologist came in to introduce herself. She had wild strawberry-blonde curls that sprang from her milky complexion. Her Irish accent was as heavy as her Irish name, Dr. Molly McSomething. Charlie's nurse introduced him to her by saying, "Look at this handsome little guy." She glanced down at him and was immediately hooked in.

"Oh, my!" she said. I looked over and noticed he was sporting a Kewpie-doll look: His jet-black locks had worked themselves into a soft little peak at the top of his head. He was alert, his midnight-blue eyes searching the room. He looked super-cool, like he'd probably misplaced a teeny-tiny, black leather jacket. Dr. Molly looked up at me and smiled warmly. "He's just the sweetest thing. You must sit here for hours admiring him. We will take really good care of him."

Then Dr. Moga came in, and my stomach swayed. "So, are we ready for this?" he asked with a soft smile. Every bit of me wanted to scream out, *No! I won't let you take him from me!* Instead, I replied sheepishly, "As ready as we'll ever be, I suppose."

Just then, Paul announced awkwardly, "It's my birthday, Doc; I need it to be a good day." Dr. Moga stared back at him, motionless.

A moment passed before he responded cautiously, "Well, happy birthday. I'm going to do my very best to make today a great day."

He sat at the side of Charlie's bed with one leg touching the floor and his hands in his lap. Then, leaning in, he said in a near-whisper, "I have some things I need to discuss with the two of you before we bring him back." His face had changed, the boy-like quirkiness harder to perceive now. He reached for a piece of paper and flipped it over to where it was clean and bare, then began to explain the sequence of the surgery. We leaned toward him to better hear his hushed words. He took extra time as he stated how hopeful he was that the movement of Charlie's single coronary artery would go smoothly. Then he started listing the surgical risks.

My stomach began swaying back and forth.

He listed infection, such as the staph which Charlie had already picked up from one of his lines in the NICU. He continued with bleeding, and blood clots. He discussed the risk of a stroke, pausing to recognize the one he'd already endured. Then there was irregular heartbeat, and the possibility of needing a pacemaker. He might not be able to come off the cardiopulmonary bypass machine; he might have trouble coming off the ventilator. Dr. Moga verbally acknowledged each little nightmare that he had written on this now-ugly piece of paper. Finally, at the bottom of the page, he added the word "Death."

No longer did my stomach sway back and forth; now it reeled, caught up in a storm of anxiety. Dr. Moga never actually *said* that last risk, as if saying the word might empower it. With his pen tracing the outline of the letters, he spoke without lifting his eyes from the page. "It's been about five years since we've lost one, a little baby girl," he said. I assumed she had had Transposition, like Charlie, and hadn't survived surgery. I didn't ask. Some things are best left unspoken.

"A hospital can pride itself on survival rates, but a lost child is a lost child. It affects us greatly," he said, his eyes once again meeting ours. "My operating room is a serious place. I want you to know that I don't play music in my OR the way some surgeons do. Nothing is taken lightly. The magnitude of the fact that I'm caring for someone's child never leaves me."

I asked him if we'd see him again, after surgery. He called over to Charlie's nurse: "Mom wants to know if she'll see me again, after surgery."

Smiling, the nurse replied, "Oh, you'll see him again! Perhaps more than you'd like!"

Dr. Moga explained that the first forty-eight hours would be crucial and that he'd be monitoring Charlie's recovery closely. "You'll see me, at all hours of the day. If you don't see me, well, I am probably on the phone calling to check on him." Extending his pen, he asked for one of us to sign the consent form for surgery. Paul took it from him and nervously scribbled across the page. With that, Dr. Moga excused himself, telling Charlie that he would see him soon. I watched him turn and walk away, and begged God to go with him.

We walked closely behind Charlie's bed as it was pushed down the hallway toward the surgical wing. There were nurses on either side of him—the small entourage necessary to move all the equipment that sustained him. For a moment, irrationally, I questioned whether we'd made the right decision in allowing him to be taken away. I'd tried hard to avoid the vision; still, my thoughts ran away with it: *a dark place, where my baby lies upon a table, his little chest splayed open with a power tool.*

Charlie's anesthesiologist led the way, her springy soft hair floating above him. My senses were ridiculously over-stimulated, as if I were walking through a brilliant dream, as if my eyelids were peeled back to take in every detail and each sound was in full stereo. The intensity of the fluorescence bounced off the stark white walls, creating an almost blinding presence of light. I felt I was walking slightly above myself. The edge between my world and that which lies beyond seemed to soften. The noise from others' lips was both loud and echoic, as if I were hearing people from a distance, but at high volume. Then the whooshing noise of wheels tracking down the hallway ended, and everyone halted in unison.

"This is as far as Mum and Dad can come," Dr. McSomething announced, her accent no longer as charming as I had thought before. I looked up at her like a lost child, my thinking and coping capacities melting into the tiles at my feet. I was helpless and vacant. I looked to her for direction. "You can kiss him goodbye for now. You'll see him in recovery once he's out of surgery."

I bent over and kissed my baby's soft, warm cheek. Paul caressed the top of his head, and we both told him how much we loved him. I took in a long deep breath, intuitively, to support my own brokenness. We stepped back from Charlie's bed, and the mechanical doors in front of him opened. Dr. Molly smiled softly at me and said, "Remember, we're going to take really good care of him." Then she helped guide him forward once again, her eyes soft and still locked in mine.

Paul and I watched them pass into the surgical unit. The doors closed behind them, and we were left standing alone. Paul kept his hand at the small of my back, as if to hold me upright.

Roller-Coasters

I don't like roller-coasters.
There, I feel better just saying it.

I've ridden plenty, and the truth is, you might not need to press very hard to get me in the seat next to you. Once it's over I'm even likely to look rather peppy, smiling and everything. But just so we're clear, I don't like roller-coasters.

My unease starts as the safety harness closes me in. Once it's in place, I check it obsessively. I push against it with all my strength, half expecting it to come unhinged. At which point, my rehearsed response (yes, I've gone over this a time or two in my head) would be an instant display of sheer, crazed panic. Hopefully my blood-curdling scream would be sufficient, and the attendant would halt the coaster, saving me from a most gruesome end.

There's still plenty to hate, though, even after I've determined I won't be thrown to my death. Like the heart-pounding unpredictability—it's ridiculous. The speed . . . well, I can say with all honesty that the speed *itself* doesn't bother me; however, having my head bounce back and forth against the safety harness, as if my neck were a rubber band—*that* I'm not a fan of. I don't appreciate the obnoxious work-up to the looming death-drop, either. All the exaggerated, persistent climbing that only ends with a terrifying free fall—it's awful.

There has got to be a payoff, though, right? It must be adrenaline surging through me, hammering inside my veins, that keeps me standing in line. I willingly give up control, and somehow I'm still breathing once the ride comes to a screeching halt. I'm dumped out on the right side of the little car, my legs behaving like silly string, and I actually feel more alive than I did before. Maybe the arousal comes from experiencing wild, raw, boundless emotion. Whether or not I liked it is trivial. Once it's over, I've been awakened.

Free Falls

*T*his part of our "ride" with Charlie—the part where we sat in an OR waiting room for hours among people dealing with ear tubes and tonsillectomies—this was the terrifying free fall. We watched doctors file in and out, informing families that all had gone well, lifting the worry from their faces. Then, with a fresh set of weepy moms, we watched the whole story unfold again. All the while I prayed, and tried to remember to breathe.

We'd endured the slow, upward climb that led us to the peak's very tippy-top. Along the ride, countless doctors' appointments had often left us with more questions than answers. There had been seemingly interminable, restless nights when I tried imagining myself with a special-needs son, wondering if I had the capacity to care for such a child. There were endless "come-to-Jesus meetings" between Jesus and me. Begging for his presence, I made certain he knew I didn't plan on doing any of this without him. I prayed for healing continuously. I prayed for the miraculous kind; I prayed for the medicine/hospital kind. All my bases were covered. By whatever means, I needed Charlie's heart to be whole.

There was time spent in meaningless thought. I didn't dwell on why this had happened to *us*. Why *wouldn't* it? Things like this happen to *someone*. Instead, I questioned whether I'd done something to cause it. Though I had followed all the "pregnancy rules," I replayed the first weeks of my pregnancy over and over in my head. I tried to remember what had filled my days, partly to find reason but mostly to clear my guilty conscience.

I was certain this was the free fall. Maybe it was all the wind in my face—perhaps that was why I had to remember to breathe. The bottom had dropped away. I could no longer see the track in front of me. All I could do was hold on tight to the harness. My core was no longer grounded. The moment I watched Charlie being pushed beyond the large mechanical doors, just as my capacities were melting into the floor, I'm certain that's when I began falling.

There was a large, empty waiting area down the hall from the small, crowded main waiting room. A nurse had showed it to us the day before. She said we might be asked to move there during our wait. The more she talked about this larger, private room, the more sugar-coated it became. She said that we shouldn't be alarmed if we were asked to move. She assured us that it didn't necessarily mean that something had gone wrong during surgery. Deciding I deserved a little sugar, I accepted her indulgences. She also wanted us to know that we didn't need an invitation to move there; the room was available to us, and we could wait there if we chose to. "Sometimes families like yours find it difficult to sit next to a distraught mother whose child is having their tonsils removed," she said, her tone pleasantly sarcastic.

I needed somewhere else to breathe, so I untangled myself from the pack and left the crowded waiting room. I walked down a quiet hallway toward the hidden room set aside for special circumstances like ours. I was curious whether anyone else was waiting there, but I found it quiet and still. Bagels and snacks were arranged, and completely untouched, on a table. The emptiness was unsettling. I stood in the doorway for a moment looking inside. I never stepped forward; instead, I turned in retreat. I'd rather huddle with the weepy ones, even if the crosses they bore paled in comparison to Paul's and mine. Their babies had been pushed beyond their reach too.

Back in the main waiting room, my mom sat closely at my side, and Paul sat across from us. He paged through magazines, nervously, rapidly. My mother took a slower approach to the distraction of "reading" issues of *Real Simple*. I sat guard, obsessively watching the door. Dr. Singh couldn't come back soon enough. "Oh, you'll be able to see it on his face," Brooke said, sitting at my other side and leaning into me. "He shows it all on his face." She stretched to peek around at the doorway into the hall. He had come in once already with an update: that Charlie was hooked up to the heart-and-lung machine and that things were moving along nicely.

The movement of his coronary artery was what haunted my thoughts. We had prayed about it that morning in the hospital's prayer chapel. One of our pastors, Kevin, had come to see us and offer prayer. We sat close to one another, knee to knee, inside the tiny chapel. Under the white light streaming down behind a cobalt-blue stained glass, we prayed that the movement of Charlie's single coronary artery would go perfectly.

Now, as Dr. Singh stepped into the crowded room, my heart tumbled from the place where it had been resting delicately. "Oh, it's good, it's good!" Brooke said quietly with a glance at his face. We stood up, enabling him to find us as his eyes scanned the room. Paul and I walked toward him as he said, "Can we step into the hall?" *Can I make it into the hallway? I can't tell what's written on his face—I might need my own heart resuscitated.*

As we huddled at Dr. Singh's side in the hallway, he said, "Everything is going very well, and he'll be coming off bypass shortly."

"And his coronary artery?" I asked.

"It went perfectly. Dr. Moga couldn't be happier."

I inhaled deeply, cleansing my body of much of the worry that had consumed it. *Thank you, Jesus, thank you, Jesus!* The words ran over and over across my mind as if a marquee were suspended within it.

Dr. Singh went back to the OR, and we were left waiting once more. I sank into my chair and allowed a smile to run across my face. "I think he's going to be all right. I do. I think he's going to be all right," I whispered.

"I think so too, honey," Paul said, smiling back at me.

When we next saw Charlie, he was lying in the middle of a full-sized hospital bed, just as he had been that morning, before surgery, except that now, blood-filled drainage tubes protruded from a large dressing covering most of his chest. He was heavily sedated. I bent down toward him in complete amazement. His skin was pink for the first time, ever. I told him how proud I was of him. I told him how happy I was.

It was as if we were seeing him for the very first time. He was not the same baby. I hadn't *noticed* that any part of him was absent before—not until this very moment. But now the part that had been missing, wherever it was, had been uncovered. We hadn't loved him any less without it, that's for certain. But he was just *different* now. He was *whole*. He was reborn.

When Dr. Moga came into the room, I wanted to run toward him and put my arms around him. I resisted for a moment, questioning the appropriateness of such an act. He smiled and said how pleased he was with how surgery had gone. My gratitude was uncontainable. I moved toward him and threw my arms around the back of his neck. I squeezed tightly and told him how thankful I was. He welcomed my embrace. Paul first extended his hand for an appropriate, grown-up handshake, but then he too threw his arm around Dr. Moga's shoulder. "Thank you, thank you, for the best birthday I've ever had!" Paul said, grinning like a child.

Dr. Moga responded by simply saying, "You're very welcome." Honestly, the whole conversation was ridiculous. Sometimes there just aren't big enough words.

Slumber Party

We slept that evening in a consultation room directly across the hallway from the surgical waiting area. The room was tiny, but it didn't have that creepy Shawshank feel to it. There were two long loveseats that faced each other from either side of the narrow room. A large dry-erase board hung on the wall above one of them. A sketch of some sort had been scribbled across it. We stood back from the drawing, trying to decide what body part it might be. We gave up quickly, deciding surgeons aren't necessarily artists. The loveseats folded open, converting into full-size beds. Someone had been thoughtful and had dropped off bedding for us.

I walked down the hallway to use the restroom before settling in for some sleep. It was dark and deserted. My only light came from a glowing exit sign hung near the junction of an adjacent hallway. The walls looked tired. I imagined them resting after the buzz of activity that filled the day. I stepped into the dark restroom. The motion sensor took a moment before the fluorescent lights flickered into use. Standing in front of the mirror, I smiled at my reflection. I was wearing jammies, but not just any old PJs—these were serious. The bottoms were Capri-length (after all, it was springtime), with skinny vertical stripes in purple, blue, and green. The top was a pretty coordinating purple with a little green bow at the neckline. Paul had seen me change and said, "You're sleeping in a closet at the hospital! Why are you dressed like you're hosting a slumber party? You couldn't find a pair of sweatpants?"

"What, you don't like my PJs?" I questioned sarcastically. "They were a gift, remember? Doug and Brooke bought them for me, for after the baby."

"Oh, they're nice, all right," he said, with his own playful dose of sarcasm. "You don't look crazy at all, walking around the hospital in them. Oh, and by the way, nice shoes." I looked down to see my white socks pulled up well past my ankles, and my black loafer-style flats on my feet.

"What was I supposed to do—bring slippers too? I am traveling light, and it's cold in here!"

He had looked back at me with his eyes wide and his chin tipped to one side—his *Well, don't say I didn't tell you so* face.

Now I did my best to quickly brush my teeth and wash my face in a public restroom. All the while, I giggled at the slumber-party girl who looked back at me.

We settled into our side-by-side beds, our faces toward each other. The light filtering under the door allowed me to see the outline of Paul's face. We chatted about what a surreal experience the day had been, and how Paul's birthday would never be the same again. We talked about missing our girl. I told him how much I loved him. We prayed for our boy, asking Jesus to continue to care for him.

Just as Paul started to drift off, I mentioned that I wasn't feeling well. My body ached, and my left breast was tender. I counted the last few days in my head, thinking I must be almost done with the antibiotics for the mastitis in my right breast. Pumping through the infection was so painful; I certainly hadn't forgotten about taking the pills—good Lord, anything to help. "You can't develop an infection while you're on an antibiotic, can you?" I asked Paul rhetorically.

"I'm sure you're just exhausted, hun," he responded drowsily. "Let's try to get some sleep."

I decided he was right, and I gave in to my fatigue. Unable to shake the heaviness of the day, I carried it with me into my sleep.

My dreams must have been crazy-intense with my heart so heavy, but whatever craziness ran through my mind didn't last long. I woke to the sound of my teeth rattling. I opened my eyes and tried to collect myself. My body was twisted around in the sheets in confusion; I was unsure of where I was. I scanned the room and found Paul's outline across from me, his body turned toward the wall. I saw the whiteboard above my bed, and with that, the memories of the last few hours flooded back to me. I searched the bed for my cell phone to see the time: 1:30 a.m. Only three hours or so had passed since I closed my eyes.

It wasn't just my teeth rattling; my whole body shook. I was cold, and I was covered in sweat. I pushed myself up to a sitting position with my legs hanging over the bedside. My purple pajama top clung to my wet body. I searched underneath it. My left breast felt fiery and rock-hard.

I sat at the bedside for a moment, thinking through what was happening. I had a fever. It was high, possibly higher than any fever I'd ever had. I was scared and disorientated. I did my best to sort out my options. I could wake Paul and have him bring me to the ER of the adjacent hospital. I looked over at him. He was sleeping hard. His breathing was deep and labored. His body begged for rest. Even if I could bring myself to wake him, I didn't think I had the physical strength to get up and move. My body was so depleted; the mere notion of walking through this building seemed too enormous.

I got up from the bed and began to rummage through our things. I found a bottle of Advil, my seemingly useless antibiotics, and a bottle of water. I struggled to open the bottles as my hands shook uncontrollably. I downed a half dozen Advil and a double dose of my nearly empty bottle of antibiotics. My body hurt everywhere, as if I'd been run over by something. I crawled back onto the pullout and wrapped myself into a fetal position. Overwhelmed by physical pain, exhaustion, worry, and, finally, self-pity, I cried and I cried and I cried.

My cries eventually quieted, and my tears began to fall across my face in silence. They cooled my fiery cheeks. I told God that this was it; I had nothing left. He must fill me up once more because I was weary; I was empty. I drifted off again, listening to the exhaustion that burdened my husband's breath.

Mad Skills

For days we sat and watched Charlie's monitors. We made it past the first fifteen critical hours, exhaling for an instant. The most precarious time was supposedly behind us. But holy buckets, mountains still loomed ahead. Scary episodes of tachycardia kept us on edge. When his heart rate rose beyond a safe threshold, alarms would sound from his monitors, bringing us to our feet. Powerless, we stood at his bedside and watched. As his numbers rose, the air in the tiny room thickened. My stomach turned. I glared back at the numbers, willing them to stop. The risk was that he could blow out the delicate stitches placed in his heart, or he could stroke out again, or he could simply go into cardiac arrest.

I was standing there alone when the worst of it happened. Danny was caring for him when the monitor sounded. The numbers rose rapidly to a level I hadn't seen before. Charlie's little body seemed pulled from me, beyond my reach, like he'd been snatched away on a wild, chilling ride. Meanwhile, I was left at his bedside standing still and forgetting to breathe. Typically cool, no-sugar Danny became nervy and unsettled. She started to pace the room, walking quickly back and forth from monitors, to IVs, to his chart, and back again. Still, the numbers rose.

Danny called for help from another nurse and started packing my baby in ice. She was gritty and steadfast. She offered me no coddling, no explanations. In fact, she hardly responded to me. Packed in ice . . . my baby boy. Then, as if his heart had pivoted, the numbers slowly began to descend. I felt him coming back closer to me; he was landing in a place I could reach once more. Danny, cool and brash, had stopped Charlie's world from spinning. I was certain she had crazy-mad skills. I had a newfound, limitless appreciation for her.

We were three days past surgery when they began to lighten Charlie's sedation. Every so often, he would wake up and open his eyes for a bit. His eyes were loopy—deliriously loopy. He seemed to scan the room, as if trying to place where he was. The narcotics were so heavy that his glossy eyes just rolled around. Then he would return to wherever his latest adventure had been, seemingly a million miles from where we were. All the while, his body lay there mending. He was on his way; we all were. (Yes, I'd been on the mend too. Pumped full of a new antibiotic, thankfully, I was moving past the mastitis.)

From the doorway of Charlie's room, I could see the nurses' station and the bay area across the PICU. One day, I noticed partitions going up around the bed where the little one lay, the baby we had seen the first time we were led through the unit. His mother was almost always at his side. She spent hours leaning against his bed, often in tears. She wasn't there now. A buzz of activity surrounded him. I asked Charlie's nurse what was going on. She told me that they were preparing for surgery here in the PICU. "Here?" I questioned.

"He's too unstable to move into the OR, so they're bringing the OR to him. If you need to walk in or out of the unit, please be as quiet as possible."

Standing in Charlie's doorway, I had a window into a private world. The partitions shielded the baby, but not the faces that surrounded him. I could see Dr. Moga's profile, and the gravity under his surgical mask. Surgical nurses stood around him in silence. From across the unit, I felt the heaviness that blanketed them. I prayed that one day that little boy would chase his big brothers, giggling as he ran after them. I pictured Jesus standing at Dr. Moga's side, the same way I had imagined him when my son lay before the doctor. I stood there watching for a moment, until the image was too heavy. I'd stumbled inside someone else's suffering. I turned away and returned to Charlie's bedside.

"Just a Few More Stitches, House."

*T*he medical drama *House* played on the TV in the OR waiting room. I hadn't seen it before, but I had heard the buzz around it: medical mysteries solved by a cocky medical god with the last name "House" and an Asperger's-like persona—the irony and timing of the show amused me as we waited. Charlie was in the OR with Dr. Moga again. Just Paul and I waited this time. There were no cheery hospital volunteers, no weepy mothers; it was just the two of us, and Dr. House. I found it refreshing. Four days had passed since Charlie was last in the OR. The large dressing over his chest had been protecting his open chest cavity. We had learned that with little ones coming out of open-heart surgery, it was routine to keep their incision open for a three- or four-day wait. It allowed swelling to dissipate and heart function to stabilize. Once the surgeon was confident that they wouldn't need to go back in, then they would close up the chest.

It was during "prime time," many hours since his surgical day had begun, when Dr. Moga closed Charlie's chest. He had been scheduled for closure earlier that afternoon, but the day unfolded into an ugly mess. What was supposed to be a simple morning procedure for a toddler had taken a scary turn on the operating table. A dicey, all-day, complicated surgery ensued. We waited all afternoon to hear whether or not Charlie would still have his closure that day. His nurse, looking at the late hour, began to prepare us for surgery tomorrow. I was frustrated at the thought of another restless night. Then, after just a few minutes more, Dr. Moga walked into Charlie's room and, with a tired grin, said, "Let's get this little guy closed tonight. I think I have enough in me for a few more stitches."

I responded with a soft, drawn-out "Really?" and hoped he heard my gratitude.

"Yes, really. We have enough staff who agreed to stay for Charlie. Let's do this tonight," he said.

Charlie's surgery was just long enough for House to solve his mystery. As the credits played, Dr. Moga came into the waiting room. "All finished," he announced. Paul and I rose to greet him, and the three of us stood in an intimate circle. Dr. Moga explained that there was now a small peak where Charlie's breastbone came together—a somewhat typical result. He also mentioned that the bottom of the incision had needed many stitches, as Charlie seemed to have an unusual loss of muscle tone there. "He'll probably want to come back to see me when he's fourteen. He'll ask if I can make things look better. I'll look much older. I'll probably have lost my hair line completely by then, and his concern will be with what girls will think of his scar." He smiled and ended with: "I'll tell him to trust me on this one . . . Girls. Love. Scars."

I put my arms around Dr. Moga one last time. The long hours of his tedious day were embedded in the sticky dampness at the crease of his neck and in the puffiness around his bloodshot eyes. I suspected he had pushed himself into this late hour, wanting to end his day sending a child into recovery.

We slept a little better that night.

Dirt Floors

I sat outside the PICU on a cushiony bench, watching the world skip by. The hospital was a project in perpetual motion, morphing one corner at a time. Some areas were bright, new, and cheery, like the vaulted entrance where I sat. Natural light poured in through the glass ceiling. Sunlight rested on people's shoulders as they came and went. The prayer chapel, with its pretty cobalt-blue stained glass, was just across from the PICU. This corner felt fresh and alive. Yet, the creepy little Shawshank room was hidden just down the hall, and the walls of the PICU, where Charlie lay, were tired and dark.

One of our pastors was coming by for a visit. Here, with the sun on my shoulders, I sat and waited for him. It was relatively quiet, even with the sounds of comings and goings and the constant movement of the large mechanical doors in the entry.

Then, like a panic alarm, her pain interrupted the quiet. The heavy, secure door of the PICU swung open. The soft-spoken Russian woman, the one who had been so kind in asking about Charlie, came barreling out of the unit, screaming and crying into her cell phone. She was hysterical, her thin body trembling. She was on the edge of something. I don't know what she was saying, or to whom, but I know what devastation sounds like. It needed no translation. Directly behind her was another heart mom, who traced the Russian woman's quivering steps. She was there for the other, just in case she needed someone to put arms around her. Our eyes met and we shared a look of heartbreak. Whatever news this woman had gotten, we had each spent our own energy running from it.

The two women sat down near me for a moment. The one who trembled hung up her phone. Still sobbing, she stood and made a beeline for the mechanical door. The other followed, glancing back at me first with a nervous look of uncertainty. I remained in the sun.

I didn't have much more of a wait before Pastor Paul arrived. He had come to pray for us, and to offer counsel, but he himself was visibly shaken when I brought him into Charlie's room. He stood back for a moment in amazement. "Oh, my. I've seen my fair share of Intensive Care, but I can say that in all my years I've never seen so much equipment, so many IVs, so much to sustain someone." He was normally a jovial, expressive man, and this was the first time I'd seen him truly troubled. As Pastor Paul, my husband Paul, and I stood close to one another at Charlie's bedside, the pastor's hand was soft with age as it nestled in mine. His prayer was hushed and gentle.

As he prayed, my mind wandered far away, to a place in Africa where Pastor Paul spends the spring of every year doing mission work: Tanzania, a place and its people that he describes as joy-filled, Spirit-filled, regardless of want and circumstance; a place that mirrors Pastor Paul's cheerful nature. There must be little ones born there too, I thought, in barren rooms, whose hearts are in need of extraordinary measures. Empathy flooded my heart again, this time for the grieving mother whose child has no privilege, where there are no specialty hospitals, only simple structures with dirt floors. My raw heart seemed to know no boundaries.

A Thousand Words

Now and then I closed my eyes to recall his face. His name was Ryan. He had fiery red, silky hair and brows. His complexion was rosy, his eyes bright blue. His face was round and his lips were slobbery, the way a perfectly beautiful, perfectly perfect nine-month-old face is. His mom sent his picture in an email. It came shortly after Charlie's diagnosis was made while he was still *in utero*, shortly after our heartbreak had a name.

Dr. Singh had assured us that once our baby recovered from surgery, things would be okay. He said Transposition was usually well managed, and he would be like every other little boy. He wouldn't have a future in the NFL or the NHL, but he would run and play with all the other kids. While I appreciated what he said, I still had trouble wrapping my mind around our impending world.

People said all sorts of things—"words of wisdom," you might say. It annoyed me. I forced a smile, knowing they had the best of intentions, but juvenile thoughts skipped through my head. *What can you possibly know about this? What do you know about anything, anyhow (insert sassy tone and internal eye roll here)?* It seemed that excessive hormones and an imminent crisis didn't bring out the best in me. But what did give me reassurance was the image of a baby boy with fiery locks. I chiseled a spot for him in my mind, making it easy to recall his sweet face when doubt crept in.

Ryan was the youngest of four children whose family lived in Massachusetts. His Transposition had gone undetected during pregnancy. He was rushed to Boston Children's Hospital immediately following his birth. His surgery now behind him, he had recovered and was beautiful. Truly, his picture was worth more than the proverbial thousand words. Ryan's sweet face was with me as we waited for Charlie. He was with me the day Charlie was born, and he remained with me as, one piece at a time, Charlie became untied.

Untangled and Untied

He had been ours for twenty days, and with the exception of the brief moment after his birth, we hadn't ever seen his face bare. I could hardly wait for the vent to come off. I wanted to get my lips on his soft cheeks. It must be instinctual. Not being able to kiss and hold and comfort was awful. It gnawed at me relentlessly. All the IVs, the monitors, the vent taped across his face, the drainage tubes—all of it became exceedingly ugly. It stood between me and this instinct, and suppressing it left me raw on the underside of my heart and my belly.

A few days past his surgery, I watched Dr. Moga's colleague, Dr. Overman, remove the drainage tubes. He was the man who had taken an early flight home to assist in Charlie's surgery. I had been hovering at Charlie's bedside a few moments before, when he came in. We chatted quietly as he examined my boy. Dr. Overman was thoughtful and reserved. He asked if I'd rather step into the hallway as he pulled out the tubes. "I'd rather stay," I said. He smiled politely and asked me to turn my head away. I was close to Charlie's side. I turned away, but not quite long enough. I had underestimated the length of tubing that had been placed under his rib cage. My stomach turned. It seemed shockingly invasive. Nonetheless, I shook it off easily; part of me had hardened in an uncomfortable kind of way.

Now it had been more than a week since Charlie's open-heart surgery and three days since the drainage tubes had come out, but still, he remained on the ventilator. Weaning him from his narcotics had left him agitated and unstable, so he had been unable to come off it sooner. He would become angry and break out in a cold, sweaty mess. His tiny body shook. He was a teeny little drug addict. We started methadone, a drug used in the rehabilitation of heroin addicts. Before we could untie him, we had to break his narcotic addiction. Just when I felt like the worst was behind us, this seemed to be the hardest part. It nearly stole my breath away.

Secrets

I wandered into Charlie's room during the wee hours one morning. His nurse was busying herself around him, chatting him up as she worked. She was intensely high-energy and seemingly unaware that it was two a.m. I startled her a bit when I strolled in. I told her I had been up pumping, and I wanted to see his little face. She smiled and said, "I think he knew his mommy was awake, because he's been wide awake too. He's been following me around the room with those eyes."

She was sweet and bubbly. Her energy could not be contained inside her petite frame. Music was playing from somewhere above Charlie. It was instrumental in a New Age healing sort of way. I was certain it was all for him. She had turned on a dim light just behind his bed; it gave off a soft glow. It was lovely. She told me how much she enjoyed caring for him, on account of how handsome and sweet he was. It seemed he'd been keeping a little secret from me: the music, the soft lighting, staying awake for the bouncy, chatty nurse. I wondered how many nights had looked like this one. It made me smile, and gratitude washed over me. I didn't stay long, knowing I'd interrupted.

Mother's Day

Charlie's vent came out the day before Mother's Day. He looked fresh and naked without it, and incredibly precious. I asked his nurse to help me remove every bit of the goopy, sticky residue from his sweet cheeks. I needed him clean and soft. With my lips to his cheeks, the rawness that had been tucked within me was cleansed.

I spent Mother's Day with him in my arms, snuggled in close. Our little Sophie came to see us too. She smelled like Tide, fresh and clean. She had damp little pigtails on top of her head. She wore a sweet, pink and white checked spring jacket and clunky, chunky little Mary Janes on her feet. She sat on my lap and I squeezed too hard, telling her how much I had missed her.

A few more nights in Intensive Care, and a few more lines removed. One more hospital floor awaited us.

Hope

I have a picture of Charlie held in Dr. Moga's arms outside of his room on the cardiac floor. The photo is blurry. He's wrapped in a receiving blanket. There are no IVs, no feeding tubes, nothing that attaches to him or ties him down. It's simply a picture of a man in scrubs holding a swaddled baby. From the first time I saw the photo, every time I see it, I find myself looking past the fuzzy image of my baby in his surgeon's arms. Instead, my eye is drawn, as if instinctively, to the wall hanging in the background. In all capital letters, it reads "HOPE."

The picture was taken the day before we left the hospital. Dr. Moga came into Charlie's room and stood at his bedside. It was the first time we'd seen him since leaving the intensive care unit. Charlie was lying in his bed, alert, eyes breathing in his surroundings. I was taken aback by the sight of Dr. Moga at first, worried that his presence meant something ominous. Dr. Singh had been by each day managing Charlie's care. I couldn't imagine that Dr. Moga made his way out of the ICU very often.

He stood for a moment in silence, studying Charlie's face. Dr. Moga was, and is, special to me. I will forever hold him in a place of absurd gratitude in my heart. As I watched him gazing at Charlie, I recognized that Charlie was special to him as well.

Dr. Moga broke the room's silence: "Okay, buddy, now you're going to have to go home and work on getting bigger, okay?" He gently ran his fingers through Charlie's dark hair, pausing where his soft spot was exceptionally concave above his forehead. Charlie was disturbingly thin. He resembled an injured, featherless baby bird that had fallen from the nest. Over his short, difficult weeks, his face had become sunken, making his big, light-filled eyes appear even more pronounced. His arms and legs were long and lanky.

"Is everything okay?" I asked, hinting toward *Why are you here? Is there something more to worry about?*

Still watching Charlie, Dr. Moga said, "Everything's great! I heard this little guy was getting ready to go home, and I wanted to tell him goodbye." Then he turned to me and said, "Thank you for letting me care for your son. It's been an honor." With a crafty smile, he added, "No offense—you and your husband seem like great people—but I don't want to see you again." We shared quiet laughter, and I said "thank you" one more time. It felt just as inadequate as all the times I'd said it before.

These last few days had been spent on a brand new, beautiful cardiac care floor. It was the hospital's newest shiny project. The first time the elevator opened to the third floor, I swore I heard instrumental music welcoming us in. It was hard to believe we were still in the same building. Each room here was private and spacious. The walls and furniture were adorned in warm blues and greens. Each room had a sofa that faced the patient bed. It converted into a surprisingly comfy sleeper. Behind the sofa was a large window that let plenty of natural light stream in. There was also a private bathroom in each patient room. Outside Charlie's room was a nurses' station and a sitting area. Zero creepy Shawshankness.

During our first couple of days on this beautiful new floor, my thoughts had still been in the PICU. I thought about the baby boy still lying in the bay, and about his weeping mommy-the one who stayed glued to her son's bedside. He was the same little one we saw when we toured the unit-the day before Charlie was moved out of the NICU. I wondered if the impromptu surgery on the unit floor had been successful. I considered the bracelet still on my wrist—the one I'd worn all this time, the physical manifestation of God's presence. I felt a nudging at my heart, yet I was reluctant. I wanted to hide the bracelet away, hoard it in a dark drawer, and pull it into the light again one day to show to my grown children, to marvel at how I cried out to God and he responded—not in thought or sentiment, but in worn silver.

I argued with the nudges. *How could I give her a bracelet that reads, "With God all things are possible" when I don't know how her story will end? What if her son never leaves this place?* I worked to push my doubts aside, realizing that I couldn't possibly begin to understand the complexities of this.

I curled up in the rocker next to Charlie's bed while he slept. It was late in the evening, and *The Tonight Show* played at low volume on the TV mounted up high across from us. I watched Jay Leno in his dark suit, both hands in his pockets, doing his nightly stand-up shtick. I was disengaged, but I appreciated the quiet company and soft noise. I was lonely.

My husband and my sweet Sophie had only left a short time ago, but I already missed them. *Just a few more nights until we'll all be tucked away together each night*—that was the thought I held close.

I hadn't committed to letting my bracelet go, but I was drawn to a pad of paper anyway. I picked it up and wrote to the mom who still sat in the ICU bay. I explained to her how I had come to have the bracelet, and what it meant to me. I told her I had seen her pain, and that I spent time praying for her and her precious son. It was late when I finished writing, and I fell asleep with the bracelet at my wrist and my arms nestled close to my heart.

Charlie woke often that night, so, finally, I brought him over to the pulled-out sleeper and laid him next to me. He traveled light now; the only thing that remained tied to him was a feeding tube taped to the side of his face. I dozed lightly on and off until the early morning.

It wasn't even seven o'clock when Dr. Singh came through the doorway into the dimly lit room. My eyes were sharp in the room's darkness. He was dressed casually in a polo shirt, spring jacket, and jeans—a far cry from his normal sharp suit and tie. On occasion he wore scrubs, and he made them look neat and tidy too. But this casual, no-scrubs, no-suit look meant it must be Saturday. He walked over to the empty bed and peered over the bed rail. He started patting around on the mattress, and then lifted up the bedding as if searching for a baby hiding underneath. It made me giggle. I didn't speak up at first, partly out of exhaustion and partly for the cheap entertainment.

Acting alarmed, he turned for the door. I called out to him, "Dr. Singh, I have him with me over here."

"Oh, thank goodness! I thought maybe we lost one!" he said, chuckling and amused with himself.

Dr. Singh sat down at the edge of the pullout. I asked him if he needed me to bring Charlie back to his bed. "No, no, this is just fine," he whispered back. With a stethoscope pulled from his jacket pocket, he listened to Charlie's heart, all the while doing his best not to disturb my sleepy baby. Dr. Singh's process was always the same: He would bow his head deeply, closing his eyes in concentration. He would work the stethoscope until he found just the right spot, and then he would listen. He would close out the world around him; you could see it falling away. It looked like meditation. He would place himself within the repetitive, distinctive, unhinged melody he heard.

When he was done listening, we chatted quietly about how Charlie's feedings were going. He needed to be eating well on his own before we could go home. As I lay on my makeshift bed in pajamas, my delicate baby snuggled in close to me as his doctor examined him, there was intimacy here. Dr. Singh—this gentle, extraordinary man—had been a stranger to us only a few short months ago. Now, his presence was entangled in our lives—we chatted, with me in jammies. He was invaluable.

Little Miss Sophie came back to the hospital later that morning. She had decided her daddy could come too. She was the big sister—a very important job. Charlie was going to get his first real bath. She *might* let Mommy and his nurse help too. Charlie's nurse had located a small step stool for Sophie. Wherever Charlie was, Sophie was right beneath him, squeezing her stool in at our feet. Then she popped up to stand tall, gaining a bird's-eye view. She found it easier that way to give us directions. "Mommy, Mommy, he's crying. . . . Mommy, Mommy, I think he's cold. . . . Careful, Mommy, please be careful." Her chocolate-colored eyes were even bigger and rounder than normal. There was so much curiosity and wonder bubbling up to her surface. Her pupils were ultra-dilated, her cheeks flushed and rosy. After Charlie's bath, she spent time holding him. It was beautiful.

A little later, Paul and I walked Sophie down to the sibling play center to play with Ms. Amy. It was her new favorite place: a staffed drop-off center for the siblings of hospital patients. The room was bright and fun. There was a big oblong table for arts and crafts, complete with paints, beads, glue, and wooden popsicle sticks. One corner of the room was for imaginary play with princess dresses, fire hats, and other costume pieces. A video game station with gaming chairs occupied the opposite corner. There were also board games, blocks, Legos, and books. Ms. Amy was part program director, part teacher, and part craft/fun organizer. She was soft-spoken, sweet, and kind; Sophie loved her. Whenever we brought her here, it didn't take Sophie long to turn to us and say, "You can leave now."

Each visit, there had been a handful of other kids here too. Sophie had made friends with one little girl in particular. She was five years old, timid, and quiet. Worry showed on her sweet little face. Her skin was dark and flawless, and her eyes were deep and blue. Her name was Indigo. Her teenage brother, diagnosed with cancer eighteen months ago, was on the Oncology floor. Sophie ran to Indigo as soon as she saw her.

"What do you want to play with today?" Sophie asked enthusiastically, jumping up and down in her Mary Janes. Indigo recoiled. Amy must have seen the concern on my face. "Oh, I'm so happy to see Sophie here again. Yesterday was a fun afternoon," Amy said. "Sophie was so persistent. She tried and tried and tried to get Indigo to play with her. Indigo finally gave in, and they had a great time together." Amy lowered her voice and said, "You have a very sweet little girl, and because of her, Indigo had a great day. Thank you for sharing her with us." With that, we left Sophie to play.

As the day inched by, I told Paul about the tugging at my heart. I showed him the letter I had written the night before and asked him what I should do, knowing all too well what his response would be: "Well, if you think that's the right thing to do, then you should do it"—followed by a quick "But if you don't want to give up the bracelet, then keep it." *Gee, honey, thanks for the insight.*

Nervously, I walked down to the PICU, letter and bracelet in hand. My heart was pounding. I felt like a thief, which I suppose was silly since I was *leaving* something and *taking* nothing. I didn't see her or her husband. The baby's nurse was chatting with another in front of the bay. Relief flooded my panicky veins. I walked into his space as quickly as possible, trying to be invisible. I didn't look at him, knowing I hadn't been invited. I placed the letter on the tray next to his bed and laid the bracelet on top. As I turned to escape, I caught the eye of his nurse. She smiled, knowing I was the mother of another patient. *Great, you have to say something now,* I thought. "I've left a little something for Mom, okay?" I said to his nurse.

"You just missed her. She stepped away for dinner." *Thank goodness,* I sighed inwardly.

"Oh, that's okay; if you could just make sure she sees what I've left." I walked away quickly, wondering why this felt so uncomfortable.

I lay on my makeshift bed that night imagining the bracelet around her wrist. I prayed for healing for her family, and I hoped my gift had been well received. Tomorrow, we would be going home.

Part IV

Embraced

We pulled up into our driveway on a crisp, sunny day. Paul turned off the car and we sat for a moment, facing our house. We lived on a cozy cul-de-sac. The front of our home sat back from the circular drive. The back of our neighbor's house was visible beside the front of ours. We were nestled in, with mature trees and landscaping providing nice privacy. It was our humble little piece of heaven on earth.

Neither of us was quick to move. I was equal parts happy and exhausted. I'd missed home. I wanted nothing more than to have my husband and my babies, together, tucked away inside our little house. Still, anxiety blanketed me too. It weighed heavily on me to bring this sweet baby with a fresh chest scar and stitches into our home.

Paul lifted Charlie's seat out of the car, carried him inside the house, and set him down in our front room. Miss Sophie had traveled in this same infant carrier. The cushion was covered in dark denim with tracings of white circus animals. I could still picture Sophie snuggled in it, but now, she crouched down next to its new occupant, cooing at him and rocking the carrier back and forth. Sophie just happened to be dressed in a dark jean jumper, making for the perfect photo op. We photographed the two of them together as sunlight poured through the picture window.

Our front picture window was the same place where I had found myself on my knees so many times over these last few months. My view had been snow-covered ground and bare, icy trees—beautiful, but barren and lonely. Winter in Minnesota isn't quick to release its grip, but once it does, spring unfolds expeditiously, like pop-up art in a children's book. Yet I had spent that pivotal moment of seasonal change behind hospital walls.

On this new day, with my baby dressed in soft fresh cotton and lying at our feet, the view from my picture window was green and lush. Our crab apple tree was in full bloom, white flowering petals decorating the full span of branches. Fallen petals blanketed the green grass under the tree's cover. The rhododendron directly under our window was covered in cotton-candy-pink blossoms. There was new life here.

That evening, while Paul and Sophie slept, Charlie and I sat and rocked in the glider in the corner of the nursery. I pulled back the curtains to see out into the evening sky. I remembered the night I had spent doing the same, after we were first told Charlie's heart was . . . tangled. Those few months ago, I had cried out asking God to see me, asking God to see him. The room that night had been in disarray, a hodgepodge of abandoned household things in need of a home. The disorder had mirrored the untidiness of my heart.

But the hysteria had passed. The room was now clean and fresh—attended to. God had indeed seen me. He had seen Charlie. He had scooped me up readily in the midst of my despair. My body—indeed, all that I was—had been burdened with exhaustion, so I gave in to him, allowing my head to drape heavily over his shoulder. Broken, I allowed him to carry me forward. His strength was unwavering beneath me. I had nestled in, finding refuge within my Father's embrace.

Charlie was mine, now perfect and whole. I changed him out of his sleeper and, before dressing him again, brought him back to the glider with me. I embraced him, snuggled him in close, his warm skin directly against mine. I put his blanket over the both of us, and we rocked back and forth. Holding him this way was everything that I'd hoped for.

Brave Enough . . . That Kind of Pain

In the midst of the confusion, in the middle of all the ultrasounds and offers of late-term abortion, Paul stood at the top of the stairway that faced down into our kitchen. I was roaming about our kitchen when he said to me, "You know, Mindy, there is the possibility that he may not survive. If it happens—if he dies—we can't let it destroy us. Please, promise me you won't let it ruin us." It obviously had weighed on him, and he was brave enough to say it out loud.

I had thought about it. *How will I explain it to Sophie? How will she ever understand?* Of course, Sophie wasn't my only concern.

What worried me the most was the same thing that weighed on Paul: What if our baby died and I couldn't find a way out of my grief? What if we ended up in such an ugly, deep place that I could never climb out? I tried to avoid daydreams about an infant funeral, but I couldn't always escape them.

What does a tiny coffin look like? Could I endure that kind of pain? My beautiful Sophie—what would the day look like to her? Paul would need a suit, I suppose. What would I wear to bury my child?

Delicate Sequins

Fifteen months later

*M*elissa wore a black blouse adorned with delicate sequins. Her slacks were simple and also black. She glistened in the darkened church corridor. Her face was wet and full of loss. Our eyes met across the room. I did my best to weave politely in and out through the crowd of her family and friends to get to her. She was trying to make her way to me as well, but she needed to stop every moment to accept condolences. I saw her daughter skipping through the crowd. She was in a puffy party dress, and giggling. Her silky dark hair bounced along with each gallop.

Once I reached Melissa, I put my arms around her and held tightly onto her. I prayed that she would eventually climb out of her deep, ugly place. What I said out loud was that I was so sorry, and that I loved her.

Zachariah had been born in December of 2005. Charlie was eight months old. Melissa's presence in our journey with Charlie had been constant. She had come to Hosanna! and laid her hands on me in prayer along with the rest of our couples group. She had whispered my name to Jesus. Months later, at Charlie's hospital bedside, she announced to me, and the rest of the group, that she was pregnant.

Brooke called on a frosty Friday morning that December. She said she had something to tell me. She had just hung up the phone with Jeff, Melissa's husband. "Melissa had her baby," she said. "It's a boy. He was born this morning. They named him Zachariah Jeffery."

"Is everything okay?" I asked, as there was a curious nervous pit in my tummy.

"Well, I'm not sure how to say this . . . there is something wrong with his heart."

"What?" I said, harshly, as if she must be cruelly making things up, because *another* baby boy born with a heart defect would be absurd.

"They think he has hypoplastic left heart," she said meekly.

"He's hypoplastic? Are you serious?" I was stunned. Hypoplastic left heart syndrome leads to a lifetime of complications and repeated surgical interventions. "Where are they?" I asked.

"They transported him from Burnsville to The University of Minnesota. Jeff is with him. Melissa is still in Burnsville."

"How can this be happening?" I asked rhetorically, knowing Brooke didn't have the answer either.

This heart thing, watching your child suffer—it was still fresh for both Brooke and me. The empathy was unbearable. Blake had just recovered from his second open-heart surgery, this time to repair a leaky valve. (At three years old, he had the most mischievous smile I've ever seen.) I had sat with Brooke in the PICU after Blake's surgery. Some of his staff recognized me as "Charlie's mom" and asked how he was doing. We explained to his nurse that, no, we hadn't met through any support groups; I was Blake's godmother, and

Brooke and I had been friends for a number of years, since before either of us had children.

Now, Jeff and Melissa? All sorts of thoughts ran through my mind, some of which were quite ugly. *They must hate us now; they probably wish that they had never come into our lives. I am marked, like a black cat. You should turn and run, because no good can come from being my friend.*

But I was also in awe of God's hand in this. How else could one explain the parallels within this small circle of friends? Even as I felt angry and manipulated, like a puppet on a string, I knew God was there. I thought about the moments spent in the prayer chapel months before. Melissa had kneeled at my feet, her intention authentic and clean. It was her petitions that remained with me. Her heart, of course, was completely unaware of the journey that lay before her.

We were able to visit Zach the week after his birth. I found two identical small stuffed puppies to bring to him. I gave our gift to Jeff and explained the reason for two. I shared how upsetting it was to have to leave Charlie's bedside at night, how I felt like I was leaving my heart with him. I told him how Charlie had one of the lions in his Isolette at all times. His nurses would use it to position tubing and IVs, and other times it was just snuggled in next to him. I kept the second lion with me; that way I felt like I had a piece of Charlie with me. I held it close to me in the night. The next evening before leaving his bedside, I would ask his nurse to switch the lions. That way, I always had his smell with me too. I hoped the puppies would provide comfort for them too.

They had a number of visitors the evening we visited. We took turns being ushered back into the Intensive Care Unit. Jeff brought Paul, Brooke, and me back to Zach's bedside. Melissa rocked him next to the Isolette. It was the first time I'd seen her since Zach's birth. I crouched down next to her. Stroking Zach's forehead, I told her how beautiful he was. He had strawberry-tinted hair and brows. His cheeks were full and round. The prominent bridge between his eyes gave way to the cutest little pug nose. His chin was pointed and sweetly dimpled. His eyes were round and attentive. I had the ability to see *him*. For me, the tubes and IVs faded away. I saw only Zach, their beautiful son.

Brooke and Doug had been able to do the same for us. They saw beyond the medicine. They noticed how much Charlie looked like his daddy.

After our visit with Zach, we chatted in a family room next to the NICU. Melissa stayed at Zach's bedside, while Jeff ushered visitors back and forth. We were surrounded by our couples group, and we talked about how unbelievable it was to be sitting in yet another waiting area of a children's hospital. Now, three of the five couples in this circle of friends faced this challenge. Incredibly, all three of us had had healthy little girls first, before these boys arrived with their tangled hearts.

Brooke and I talked with our friends about how fantastic Zach's color was, and how nice it was that he was stable enough to be held. Kelli came back from the NICU and sat down quietly next to me. She was half of the fifth couple. After a number of years of marriage, and going back and forth with the decision of whether or not to have children, Kelli and her husband, Ben, had recently welcomed a healthy boy, whom they named Ethan.

I looked over at her to see streams of tears running down her face. It looked as if a faucet had opened under her heavily made-up eyes. It took me by surprise, as there was no sound to accompany her pain. I opened myself up to her by extending my arm around the back of her chair. She looked at me and calmly said, "I just don't understand why someone so small has to suffer that way. All I could see when I looked at Zach was my Ethan. It would be horrible to see him like that—all those tubes and IVs coming from everywhere. I just don't understand it . . . I don't understand this at all." She looked at both Brooke and me and said, "I can't believe the two of you had to watch your sons like that. How could you do that?" Her tears continued to flow down her face and drip gently from her chin. We had no words to answer her, nor did she expect any.

Irrational or not, anxiety loomed among us concerning possible future pregnancies for the other two couples. And indeed, other challenges would come. A year later, we would surround Chad and Kendra in prayer when Kendra experienced a massive uterine bleed during her second pregnancy. After weeks of bed rest, she delivered, much to her obstetricians' surprise, a healthy baby boy. They named him Caleb, which means "faith," "devotion," and—appropriately, but unintentionally—"whole-hearted."

Melissa took a break from Zach's Isolette and joined us in the waiting room. We sat and watched her open baby gifts and talked about Zach's upcoming open-heart surgery, the first of three he faced in his first three years. They would be followed by an eventual heart transplant in early adulthood. Melissa struggled over the sweet little outfits. Running her fingers across them, she said she hoped Zach would wear them someday.

After a short while, we gathered around Melissa and Jeff in prayer. We prayed for healing. We prayed for Zach's doctors and his nurses. We prayed for peace and strength for Zach's mommy and daddy. And we prayed for their daughter, Gabby, at home. We each took our turn petitioning. I felt flushed and warm, the same way I had in the prayer chapel months before. Light penetrated my eyelids, even in the darkened room.

Then Jeff began to pray. His voice was rich and beautiful. The first night we had met, after listening to him read, I complimented him on how beautiful his voice was. I told him he sounded like a broadcaster, and that he should be on the radio. Melissa smiled, saying that he had studied radio broadcasting in college. Jeff smiled too, but offered no response. Jeff isn't chatty. He's even a bit "greedy" with his words, which is to say that he saves them for the big stuff. He isn't greedy with his smiles, though; those he gives out generously.

Jeff prayed for healing for his son, expressing openness to however healing might come. He prayed for miraculous healing; he prayed for medical healing through the hands of Zach's doctors and nurses. He prayed that Zach would be continuously surrounded by the presence of Jesus and his angels. Lastly, he prayed that God's will be done. He prayed that Zach's heart would be made whole and perfect. And he prayed for Zach to be free from pain, even if that meant losing him. His faith astonished me, while his courage brought me to a place of both admiration and of fear.

I don't ever remember surrendering to the will of God the way Jeff did in that moment. I admired him. The room overflowed with emotion.

I made my way over to Melissa. I held her for a very long time, and we wept together. It was the same embrace Brooke had for me in the prayer chapel, when we gathered to pray for Charlie. I held Melissa close to me, and in that moment, it wasn't Zach's heart I wept for; it was hers.

Zach's first and most critical surgery was a success. They were given hope for his progress, and they waited on his recovery. We hosted the couples group at our house during that time. We weren't sure whether Jeff and Melissa would join us for our biweekly "let's chat, eat, pray, and laugh together" meeting, but we hoped that they might take a break from the hospital. I heard our guests starting to arrive, and as I came down the stairs into our entryway, I saw Charlie in Melissa's arms.

She was swaying intimately with him, back and forth, and kissing his round cheeks. Tears streamed down her face. She looked up at me and said, "We are having a little moment here; I hope its okay. I'm imagining better days ahead for us, for Zach and me." I imagined that for her too.

Each time we visited Zach in the hospital, his color was beautiful. He was alert and strong. But as the weeks went by, Zach seemed to take two steps backward for every step forward. Each time he was brought off his ventilator, he struggled to breathe on his own, and they were forced to re-intubate him.

One evening after leaving the hospital, Jeff and Melissa received a late-night phone call. It was Jeff's mom, who was staying at the hospital with Zach that evening. She wanted them to know that Zach's breathing had become so labored that they were going to have to put him back on the ventilator. Just moments later, she called back, hysterical, telling Jeff that she thought they were losing him.

Later, Melissa described a frantic, dangerous midnight car ride back to the hospital. They arrived to find their little boy unresponsive. His room was filled with medical staff working frantically to resuscitate him. They worked on his tiny body for an hour and a half. Finally, they admitted to Jeff and Melissa that their efforts weren't working. They continued for just a short time more, ceasing at Jeff's request. "You can stop now; it's okay," Jeff said. "He's not here anymore; he has already been escorted home."

Melissa and Jeff spent time with Zach after his passing. They rocked him and sang lullabies. They were able to hold him close, yet Melissa would describe emptiness, both consuming the room and in her arms. He wasn't there; he was indeed home.

Jeff's entry on Zach's CaringBridge site, written just hours after his passing, read:

Thank you Jesus, our Lord, for never leaving Zach's side. Thank you for walking him into heaven and without any pain. He was always yours and you lent him to us to be stewards for the 9 months of pregnancy and the 6 weeks of life that he had. Praise be to God; Amen!!

Hundreds of people packed into the church where Jeff and Melissa were now members to honor Zachariah. Melissa was an elementary school teacher in the community where they lived, and they were active in their church, so the family was well known. Though Zach's stay on earth was just six short weeks, he had touched the lives of so many. Their pastor spoke of Zach's heart being whole in the arms of Jesus. He highlighted Luke 18:16 (New International Version): "But Jesus called the children to him and said, Let the little children come to me, and do not hinder them, for the kingdom of God belongs to such as these."

Zach was buried next to Melissa's cousin's son, who had died only months before. Melissa found solace in having him near little Tanner. We stood at their gravesites, shivering in the damp frostiness of late January. I thought about the puppies I had given Jeff, at the hospital, just a few weeks ago. One of them was nestled inside Zach's coffin. Quietly, we sang "Jesus Loves Me" to Zachariah, and released hundreds of white balloons into the sky. We stood watching them drift off, further and further away, finally fading into the distance.

Melissa struggled to leave the side of his tiny white coffin. She was his mommy; how could she walk away and leave him here in the cold? Finally, Jeff guided her back to their car.

We picked up our kids from Paul's parents' house later that evening. We held them longer, and squeezed them tighter, than usual. As we drove home, Paul and I chatted quietly in the front seat. We talked about the enormity of the day. We didn't need to express the obvious to each other—how close we came to losing our own son. We talked about why God would bring us into this circumstance, and what we were meant to do now (questions like *What am I supposed to do with Zach's passing? What does God need from me? What if I can't figure it out? What if I figure it out but I fail anyway? What kind of a friend can I be to Melissa now?*).

I struggled with how to be supportive of Melissa and Jeff. God's presence was overwhelming, and if I'm honest, it was frustrating. I felt he was asking something of me, but I didn't know what it was. I felt special and touched and completely unworthy, all at the same time. Did he really know who I was? Did he make some sort of mistake in this? I had called out to him in my worst hour and he was there—with jewelry, for heaven's sake! Now what? It was easy to be supportive to Brooke and Doug, whose sick baby had gotten stronger and survived. But how could I do the same for Jeff and Melissa? How could any of us? They were in a place of grief that I didn't understand. I wanted to get it right.

My mind and my heart raced, and then I heard this little voice from the back seat: "God is in control." I turned around to see Sophie strapped into her booster chair, smiling at me.

"What did you say, honey?" I asked.

I had heard her clearly the first time, but I needed to hear it again. So she repeated herself, only this time she added a little giggle and said, "You know what I mean, Mommy. God is in control."

I stared at her intently. I asked her where she had heard that before. She shrugged her shoulders and threw her hands in the air, as if to say, "What do you want from me? I'm only three!"

Paul and I looked at each other with wide eyes. It was in that moment that I remembered Sophie telling me, months before, that Melissa's baby would be born with a *special heart.* "Just like Charlie and Blake's heart, Mommy," she had said. I tried to correct her at the time, explaining that not all babies had *special hearts.* She argued the point with me, and finally I gave up in frustration. It wasn't the first time things like this had happened with Sophie. She knew things, in a way I couldn't explain.

I decided that Sophie's little voice from our back seat— "You know what I mean, Mommy. God is in control"—was yet another gift, another piece of "jewelry" from heaven. I cherished it. It has helped me let go of anxiety, and all of the self-doubt that swirled around Zach's death. Resting in "God is in control" made all the difference.

Melissa needed to take a step back from her friendship with Brooke and me. I respected her decision. Seeing Charlie and Blake thriving was simply too difficult for her. I prayed for healing—that they would climb out of their despair and find joy again.

Incredibly, Zachariah, a name chosen for their little one before his birth, is Hebrew for "the Lord remembers." The Lord remembered Zachariah, Jeff and Melissa's heaven-bound boy—and so would I. His imprint is forever on my heart.

Drunken Stagger

"Sleep is for the dead." That's what Paul's grandfather always said, and for two years it was our household motto. Paul abandoned ship early on. He settled onto the sofa in our family room the week we were home from the hospital. The aged yellow leather was soft and cool, and the room was quiet. After some weeks had passed, Paul would announce that he was going to *couch* instead of going to bed. He tried to elicit sympathy about being thrown out of his bedroom by a pint-sized man, but he'd left of his own free will. He might have been sleeping on the couch every night, but at least *he* was sleeping.

For over a year, Charlie woke every two hours, and was nearly two years old before he slept for four or five hours at a time. His little nervous system seemed to be remarkably overstimulated. He had such a difficult time settling, and he was easily startled. Each time he woke, he seemed to search for me, making sure he hadn't been left alone. Giving in to my exhaustion, I kept him at my side. Every attempt we made to settle him into his crib was to no avail. He cried and cried and cried. We listened from the hallway, trying to resist his pleas. Then, inevitably, one of us would cave, giving in to our fear that he had worked himself into a dangerous place, heart-wise. The age-old advice "Just let him tire out; it's okay to let them cry" just didn't seem to fit. How long does one let a baby with a zipper scar and a tenacious temper cry?

Charlie had won the battle. Charlie – 700 points; Mommy and Daddy – 0.

Charlie was nearly a year old before he started crawling. He worked painstakingly hard for each milestone, making each accomplishment sugary sweet. First, he worked his way into a modified army crawl. His left side dominated and led the charge ahead; his right side was slightly tucked in and favored. At fourteen months, he was up on two feet—well, some of the time. It was a sideways, drunken stagger, with more tumbling than might usually be expected from a new walker. Stairs proved especially challenging. He wouldn't attempt them unless he could hang on to the railing, and only by leading with his left side. He'd turn his body and walk down sideways, his left arm crossed up and over his chest so that his hand never left the railing. It was our flashing-red warning light that not all was well: His stroke had left its mark.

It would have been easy to scoop him up and carry him; he was tiny enough, that was for sure. Instead, we stood and watched painfully as he struggled, knowing he'd have to work through it on his own. We stood close enough to catch him in mid-tumble. Yet, it infuriated him. I'm not sure what upset him more: the fact that he couldn't get his body to do what he wanted, or that we were there seemingly anticipating his failure.

Words came late too. When Charlie was three years old, we sat for the first time in a busy therapy center waiting room. Trees and frogs were painted on the walls, and children's creative, if unrecognizable, artwork hung proudly in rows. Pediatric Speech, OT, and PT therapists, often bare-foot, always full of energy, came in and out of the room in a constant stream. There was chatter about the success and frustration of that day's session, and then on to the next waiting child.

Walking through the door was like entering a brave new world. The walled-off, internally focused expressionlessness of autism; the affectionate cherub faces of Down syndrome; indiscernible speech from a child with an otherwise ordinary appearance; a tiny pink wheelchair; a young boy with a disfiguring burn—all in this place. Little people moved forward into each new day, giving little regard to others' perceptions about their deficits. It wasn't the place of woundedness that one might imagine. It was filled with quirkiness, chaos, and accomplishments.

Charlie pushed his words out of one side of his adorably sweet, mischievous little monkey mouth. It wasn't always apparent, but certainly more so when he was tired—a likely manifestation of the stroke. Half the time, I watched him with a heart of concern, and the other half, I was thinking it was the cutest thing I'd ever seen. His speech therapist, Annie, fell in love with him. She was young, blonde, and kind. Her face lit up when she came to find him. They worked hard, and she laughed at his unusual, dry sense of humor (yep, even at age three, he would insinuate a joke and, instead of laughing at it, would tip his head to the side and raise his brows).

OT and PT evaluations came, and therapy too; Charlie put everything he had into any test before him. When a task deemed especially difficult, he turned up the charm. Ah, charm was an area where he had no deficiencies, no shortages, and he poured it on.

I'm Four, Fear Not

He was standing at the poolside, anxiously waiting his turn. Water poured down his legs, as he had just hoisted himself up and out at the side of the pool. It took him longer than the others, but he did it all the same. His swimming trunks hung down with the weight of the water. His orange Speedo goggles were pressed tightly around his eyes, rubber straps wild off the side of his face. His eyes looked big and buggy under the distorting plastic lenses. He stood between two little girls, one in an actual yellow polka-dot bikini, the other wearing, well, pink, of course. The three of them giggled as their teacher sang and splashed them from the pool. They bounced with excitement, waiting to hear their name in the song about froggies jumping in. It would be their cue to jump off the side and into the water.

I watched from a distance, my heart pounding with anticipation. I had a feeling this time would be different—this time he'd go for it. I could see the excitement bound up in his body. He heard his teacher's cue, and for the first time, Charlie jumped in. He jumped without consideration, feet first, full force, no holding back, fearless. My emotion poured out onto my cheeks. He came up and out of the water and into his teacher's arms with a joker's smile. Holding him, she turned to me and smiled. He had put his fear behind him. It may have been a bit harder for him, but he had decided to jump anyway. Amid the yellow polka-dot bikini and the iridescence shining off the water's surface, I recognized his adversity, but more importantly, I saw his amazing achievement—and all that he is. I saw *Charlie*.

Seeing Sophie

*W*hile Charlie was learning to jump in with both feet, Sophie was finding her way in the first grade. She was bright, social, and beautiful. She loved school; it was her favorite place to be. As she navigated her world, she did so with zero sense of urgency—zero. I'm not sure exactly what went through her pretty little dark-haired head, but I suspect it sounded something like: "Mom, settle down already, we'll get there soon. They aren't going to start any of the fun stuff without *me*." While on occasion I appreciated her laid-back, free-spirit sensibilities, a recent letter from the school's social worker about her frequent tardiness had my nervy attention.

Like most mornings, on this particular winter day we watched the school bus drive past our house, so I loaded the kids up in our frosty minivan. We pulled up to the school among dozens of other hurried families dropping kids from the passenger side of their vehicles. We waited our turn behind a handful of other minivans. As we inched closer, I reminded Sophie that she had to *hurry* to get to her classroom before she was marked tardy again. "Have a great day, Sophie! I love you, and please *hurry!*" I said as she opened the sliding door.

"Okay, Mom. I love you too. Bye, Char-Char," she said.

"Bye, Hot-dog. I love you," Charlie said, waving from his booster seat. She rolled her eyes, shook her head, and slid the door closed. I watched her *stroll* toward the school entrance as other kids bustled past her. I smiled and thought, *This is how she was made, God help me.*

Sophie was a few feet from the door when she stopped and turned. Instead of going into the building, she started walking toward the school bus lane. Most buses had pulled away, except for the one equipped with a wheelchair lift at the end of the line. *What is she doing?* I watched her walk to the remaining bus, just as her classmate, Ella, was lowered to the ground.

"Let's go, Mommy!" Charlie demanded from the back of the van. Enthralled, I couldn't pull away. Vehicles started to move around me. I rolled down my window, straining to hear through the icy breeze.

Ella's para smiled at Sophie and said, "Good morning, Sophie. How are you?"

"I'm good! Hi, Ella!" Sophie said as Ella's chair was rolled off the lift.

Ella's face lit up as she worked out a stammered "Hi, Sophie!" She was tiny. Her hair, mousy blonde, was thin and silky. Thick, oval-lensed glasses sat upon her petite, sweet face. She struggled to lift her head up and make eye contact with my girl. A pink blanket was tucked under her legs, her backpack slung around the back of her wheelchair. The three of them—Ella, Sophie, and Ella's para—made their way toward the school entrance. Sophie walked close to Ella's chair, manipulating the hand control for her. She did so comfortably, like she'd helped her a dozen times before. I could no longer hear their voices in the wind, but I could see their chatter and laughter.

Sophie truly *saw* Ella, while I *saw* Sophie.

Baby's Breath

*S*ome days I forgot. I know it sounds ridiculous, but Charlie was like any other child. With the exceptions of an occasional tumble and his empathetic intuition, especially in matters of suffering, he was like any other child. Zipper scar to boot, we moved on into our days busying ourselves with the things young families do. Then there were other times—less frequent, but more powerful—when I considered all he had endured and how easily things might have ended differently. Perhaps Charlie's empathetic nature wasn't so unexpected after all. Since leaving the hospital with my boy, my heart seemed exposed, raw even, to the trials of others.

When Charlie was eighteen months old, a mom from Michigan found our CaringBridge page. Liz was expecting a Christmas baby. She chose the name Charles because of its meaning: "Strong Man." Her Charlie would share the same heart defect as ours. She expressed that we gave her hope. I prayed for her Charlie's heart. I prayed for her heart too.

The week after Thanksgiving, Liz's water broke and her baby came early. He was small, and his lungs were underdeveloped. He spent his first evening in critical condition. Like our Charlie, her Charlie underwent a septostomy. As he began to recover, Liz and her husband looked ahead to his open-heart surgery. But the evening following the septostomy, his blood pressure began to drop, and he went into cardiac arrest. Their five-pound baby suffered a heart attack. He was three days old when, in Liz's words, "He went home to the Lord." Their loss weighed on me.

Charlie wasn't the only angel I thought about. The memory of Melissa's Zachariah was ever-present. And there was still another: Stacey was a sonographer. She found her baby's heart defect herself, an experience I could hardly imagine. We connected on Facebook. A simple message to her on a support page, telling her I would pray for her baby, sparked an online friendship. She was in the middle of a pregnancy with more questions than she could find answers to. She lived in St. Cloud, an hour and a half north of Minneapolis. Dr. Singh would be her baby's doctor, and she planned to deliver at Abbott. A team from Children's would wait for her baby, just as they waited for Charlie.

Though we never met, still my thoughts were often with her. As the image of Ryan, the baby boy with fiery red, silky hair and brows, had helped me so, I hoped to be a picture of hope for her journey. For weeks we messaged back and forth. I listened to her fears, and I prayed for her. Her delivery was scheduled, and I spent that spring morning thinking of her. Her sweet Gaven lived for thirty-two hours. In addition to a heart defect, he had kidney and lung trouble.

When their hope had run out, Gaven's nurse removed all that tied him down and placed him in Stacey's arms. Later, she beautifully expressed feeling Gaven's breath against her skin. It was a moment she had thought about each day of her pregnancy, ever since the moment she knew he was hers. His breath against her skin, she said, was all that she dreamt it would be.

The evening of Gaven's memorial service, I crawled into Charlie's bed with a heavy heart. Stacey's loss had opened up a dark place for me. Even though Melissa was the only one I had put my arms around, thoughts of these lost baby boys and their mamas' broken hearts chased me. Charlie slept peacefully in our quiet house. As he lay on his back with his arm extended up on his pillow, I snuggled in close and gently rested my head on his chest. I listened to the rhythm of his heart. With my face below his, I closed my eyes and let his breath fall upon my cheek.

Fight or Flight

As Jesus was walking along, he saw a man who had been blind from birth. "Rabbi," his disciples asked him, "why was this man born blind? Was it because of his own sins or his parents' sins?" "It was not because of his sins or his parents' sins," Jesus answered. "This happened so the power of God could be seen in him." —John 9:1-3 (New Living Translation)

"Jesus is in my heart, so why can't I see him on the x-ray? Why?" We were five years in with Charlie, and this was a parenting moment you can't possibly prepare for. Cardiac x-rays, echocardiograms, bottles of antibacterial foam mounted on the walls for easy access—it all stirred up fear. We waited nervously in an examination room, hopeful for that moment when Dr. Singh said, "You look great. Go do all the things that little boys do. Be nice to your big sister, and we'll see you back in a year."

Dr. Singh popped into the room and said, "Hey, buddy, how are you?" He apologized for our wait and said to Charlie, "Do you think you could come down the hall with me to meet a baby?" He looked over at Paul and me and said, "There's a family down the hall with a new baby. The mom is upset. I can tell her it's going to be okay, but she won't really hear me. Seeing this bruiser here might make a difference."

We followed Dr. Singh down a hallway and into another examination room. She sat with her back up against the wall. I never saw her baby, as he was tightly wrapped and tucked close to her chest. Her body protected him as if he were threatened here. It looked like "fight or flight" had kicked in, and she was prepared for either. The emotion that covered her face was heart-wrenching. I smiled at her, but she didn't see me. Her eyes were fixed on Charlie. She gazed down at him, as if he were the only little boy she'd ever seen.

Dr. Singh said, "This is Charlie."

"Hi, Charlie!" the woman said to him, her voice wild.

He responded with an unusually shy "Hi." Normally very social and chatty, Charlie seemed uncomfortably aware of all the raw emotion here.

"Look, buddy," I said, "they have a brand new baby. Can you believe you were that tiny once too?" Paul introduced himself to the dad, who sat against the opposite wall.

"Charlie had open-heart surgery when he was just a baby," Dr. Singh said, smiling down at Charlie. You could see the wheels turning in her head. Her eyes never left Charlie's face. He didn't look anything like the weak image she'd shaped in her mind. Glimpses of hope challenged her troubled emotions. "He's doing fantastic!" said Dr. Singh.

"Well, you sure look great, buddy," the dad said with a smile. He looked at Charlie, and then back at his troubled wife.

I looked to her and said, "I know this is scary, but you're in really great hands. Dr. Singh is the very best." We congratulated them on their new baby and turned to leave.

She wiped the tears from her face and said, "Thank you for coming to see us, Charlie."

"You're welcome. Bye," he said with a polite wave. She watched his every step. He put his hand in mine, and we turned and walked away.

Opalescence

Lord, make me a rainbow, I'll shine down on my mother. She'll know I'm safe with you when she stands under my colors . . . what I never did is done. —"If I Die Young," by The Band Perry

*B*rooke and I stood anxiously at the end of a long line of people tucked inside the church's bright corridor. We could see him ahead of the crowd, warmly welcoming each embrace. He wore a dark suit and cradled a vibrant lilac-colored urn in one arm. Natural light poured down from the skylights in the vaulted ceiling. It bounced off the opalescence of the urn. It was beautiful, just like our friend Kelli.

As we inched our way toward him, I noticed a funeral director come and whisper into his ear. Ben let the man take the urn from where it had been nestled against his jacket. He turned and walked away with it tightly secured between both hands. Ben continued to greet people who had come with condolences. It was difficult to look away from him; my disbelief was paralyzing. I studied his face.

The day he lost her, his capacities must have melted into the floor beneath his feet. They must be gone, leaving him helpless and vacant. Having experienced the melting away of my own capacities, knowing what vacancy and helplessness felt like, I now recognized it in Ben.

Ben had received a phone call at work asking him to come home. There had been an accident. I imagined their morning had probably been like any other. Ben shared how Kelli, and the light of their world, Ethan, sent him off to work each and every day. Waving from their front stoop, they said, "We love you, and we like you, Daddy." Over and over they repeated it—"We love you, and we like you, Daddy"— until Ben's car disappeared in the distance. Kelli's intention was to teach Ethan that it wasn't only important that people knew they were loved, but that they were liked too.

It was a perfect August morning. The sky was bare, bright, and blue. Ethan, sweet and full of adventure, was, without doubt, excited for his first day of Nature Camp. Kelli loaded him up in her SUV, along with their two collies, Jack and Tenison. Tenison, known simply as "T," was their younger, spunkier, "the pup never left him" collie. Jack was their mature, slow-moving firstborn. Jack had done his best to accommodate the arrivals of both T and Ethan.

They set off for the pretty drive outside of town. Farmers' fields lined the curvy country highway. The air here was fresh. Kelli had fallen in love with Northfield, a small, artsy college town not far from Minneapolis-St. Paul. They had built a busy little life here. She was an affectionate, engaged kind of mommy. Ethan had become the center of her world. As she dropped him off, she undoubtedly gave him a squeeze. She would have encouraged him to enjoy himself and told him she would be back to pick him up in the afternoon.

Kelli had a friend in every room. She had a way of connecting with people in every area of her life. Her friend Brenda was also there that morning, dropping her daughter off at camp. Noticing that Brenda's daughter was struggling with some separation issues, Kelli waited for her friend. They walked out to the parking lot together, chit-chatting the way young mothers do. "You're a good mom, Brenda, and she's going to have a great day," Kelli said to her, smiling reassuringly. With that, she turned and made her way back to her SUV, where T and Jack waited.

Kelli never wore a seatbelt. Her decision to skip the belt seemed amiss. She was an otherwise intentional, thoughtful person. She was obsessively, crazy-decisive. She practiced and taught yoga. She was a vegetarian. Ethan ate whole organic foods. They didn't watch television because she was worried about the negative influence it might have on their family. Decisions weren't made hastily.

A conversation we had had about her seatbelt habits stuck with me. Kelli had stood in my kitchen a handful of years ago as we prepared for one of our chatty small-group nights. She announced that she was expecting, and we were over-the-moon excited for her. "Now I suppose Ben is really going to be on my case about my seatbelt," she said.

Taken aback, I asked her about it: "You seriously don't wear a seatbelt?"

In a very non-apologetic, Kelli-like way, she said it made her feel too restricted, too confined. "I'll put it on if I'm riding in a car with Ben, just because he is so insistent about it," she said.

It was a single-car accident on a curvy country road. She simply lost control, distracted by something. The tire marks indicated her initial swerve, and then her ill-fated overcorrection that sent her SUV rolling like a tin can into a farmer's field. She was thrown from the vehicle, along with Jack and T. The first person to come upon the scene found her lifeless, along with their beloved Jack.

We didn't find out about the accident until the following day. Paul called me at work, explaining that Brooke had called, panic-stricken. Kelli had been killed in a car accident. In my own disbelief I decided that it wasn't really *our* Kelli. It was a mistake, simply an unfortunate misunderstanding. I quickly searched the internet for an auto accident in Northfield, sure I would find the name of someone else's friend. My search brought up a short article stating that a single-car accident had resulted in the death of a 36-year-old Northfield woman.

I made a nervous phone call to Ben. He answered, and I told him how sorry I was. I waited for him to ask me what I was talking about and to hand the phone over to Kelli. Instead, he said, "It's just awful, Mindy. It's just awful. She is my whole world." There it was—this was really happening. As we spoke, he was on his way to look at Kelli's vehicle. He said that Jack had been found at the accident scene with Kelli, but Tenison was still missing. He wanted to see if there were any signs of his remains in the SUV.

I told him that we were here for him. I told him that if he found himself needing anything at all, to please call. It sounded diminutive and stupid, even as it came from my mouth. What could I possibly do for him? What he needed was his wife, his life partner. He needed Ethan's mommy. He needed to find his son's dog. He needed strength to restore his melted capacities.

The line inside the church's corridor dwindled, and we found ourselves facing Ben. We put our arms around him; I was at his right and Brooke at his left. We hung on to one another the way only close friends can. He repeatedly said, "It's going to be okay. It's going to be okay." We continued to hold him up, and soon his statement turned. "Isn't it going to be okay? It is going to be okay, isn't it?" I offered him no words. Instead I wept into the shoulder of his suit jacket.

We found our seats inside the church. Our couples group sat tightly woven together. I wrapped my arms around Kendra; her face was wet with pain. She'd connected with Kelli through the years the way I had with Brooke. Her loss was profound.

Melissa and I embraced. In my emotional feebleness, I thought only of her lost son. I sat, and memories of Zach's funeral flooded my mind. I was taken back to his day, three and a half years earlier. I saw Kelli there. She was restless and nervy. Her tension was so immense; I saw it stacked across the prominence of her shoulder blades.

Kelli wore her heart on the outside, visible to the world. She exposed her fears. She hadn't ever witnessed death, making this baby boy's funeral her first to attend. Certainly we were all anxious that day, but Kelli was dressed in her anxiety. She stayed close, careful not to leave our side. She questioned the sequence of the day, like a worried child.

Kelli asked that Brooke and I stand with her to view Zach's body. We waited behind pairs of people who were doing the same. The line moved more quickly than I liked. In an instant, we were the ones closest to him. Together, we reluctantly stepped forward. He was dressed in a sweater-and-hat set, tightly knitted in pale blue with white detailing. It was precious. The outfit was a gift from Brooke and Doug, a "welcome, baby" gift brought to the hospital during our visit. It was one of the outfits Melissa had heavy-heartedly hoped he would get to wear. Now, he lay in a bassinet with soft lace skirting. He was free of tubes, wires, and tape. Nothing tied him down any longer. We stood in silence, holding onto each other. There were no sufficient words.

Kelli's own son, Ethan, was just six months old when Zach died. Viewing the body of a baby boy not much younger than your own sends you to an inconceivable place. Empathetic fear is so palpable, so commanding, in a room that mourns the young. It seemed to devour oxygen, making the air thick and difficult to breathe.

That same heaviness filled the church during Kelli's funeral as we mourned her on this day. The misty eyes of adult men surrounded me. Paul sat close to my right. He inhaled deeply, searching for oxygen to cleanse his troubled heart. "This is my worst nightmare," Paul said. "Ben is living my worst nightmare, that you would leave one day to run an errand and you would never come home. I would be alone, and my children would be without their mother."

Emotion overwhelmed this space. It was stacked into the openness above us, reaching upward even beyond the vaulted ceiling. Yet, in this space heavy with darkness, there was light too.

Light came from the sweet voice of the young girl who sang Mercy Me's song "I Can Only Imagine." Her innocence poured into the room like cool spring air through an open kitchen window. It flowed over the light in Ethan's face. This day changed his story, yes, but even so, a lifetime of promise was before him.

Dressed in a crisp pastel-striped dress shirt and khakis, he sat fidgeting in the front row. The significance of this day reached far beyond his four years. He was playful with his puppy Tenison, who sat at his feet. Not all was lost that day. Thankfully, Tenison had survived the accident and, after being gone for three days, had made his way home. Light came from that too.

Kelli's presence here was impressive. Her spirit, no longer confined within the constraints of her physical body, moved over us. It was everywhere, above and between us. It stirred within this raw, emotionally charged space. The light of all that she was, her opalescence, shined, and I could see it.

White Candles, White Balloons

Today was All Saints Day. I watched people make their way to the front of the church. Hundreds of white candles adorned tables and partitions that faced the congregation. The stories they carried forward didn't exactly look like sad ones. Rather, they looked like hearts somewhat mended with time's passage. Paul sat at my side, while Sophie and Charlie were off at Sunday school. Our pastor had taken the time to read the names of church members who had passed since the church's inception, more than thirty years ago. She had announced each name with intent, giving pause before moving on to the next.

The congregation was then invited to come forward to light a candle in memory of a loved one. I was content with sitting and watching the polite mass of people make their way forward. Remembering this same time last year, I was amazed at how quickly a year had flown by. The year prior, I had made my way forward to light a candle for Kelli. It was just a few months after her death, and the rawness of her loss was still etched into my heart. Sitting there a year later, I wasn't thinking about eternity or the people I'd lost. I wasn't having a spiritual moment. I was merely thinking, *Holy buckets, a whole year . . . gone.*

It snuck up on me, really. A woman with her teenage son caught my eye. I watched the two of them make their way to the front. She had her arm around the back of him, guiding him forward the way mothers do; only, he towered above her. They paused for just a moment and then lit their candles together. I found it endearing, and I closed my eyes. I saw Kelli with a boy upon her knee. It was Melissa's son, Zach. The image settled in my mind's eye. Kelli looked beautiful, her dark, full locks falling around her face. Perched upon her lap, Zach had a tint of strawberry running through his golden hair. He'd grown from a frail newborn into a happy young boy. They were holding onto each other, tenderly, the way a mother holds a son. The image took my breath away. I hadn't considered it before that moment: The time will come when Kelli will hold her own son again. Likewise, someday, Melissa will scoop up her son in her arms. But for now, and in these moments, Kelli and Zachariah held onto one another.

I thought about the moment when I had watched tears flow silently down Kelli's face the day we visited Zach. She was moved by his suffering and at a loss for understanding. I saw her at Zach's gravesite too, clinging tightly to Ben with one arm, while holding white balloons to honor Zach in the other. I watched her release them into the brisk winter air, her gaze lifted toward the sky.

Riding in Cars

The soul is healed by being with children. —Fyodor
Dostoyevsky

We were out for a drive through the city, my babies and
me. The day was sunny and fresh. With the windows
down, cool air blew through the Jeep's cab. A voice from the
back interrupted our cruising music: "Sophie, why did my
tubes get crossed up? I mean, how did that happen to me?"
My finger promptly hit the off button on the radio. Charlie
was five, and he preferred to ask the big questions of his big
sister first. I suspect he figured he was more likely to get it
straight from her. I was on edge. I hoped she would answer
him well. He believed her every word. If Sophie said it, then
it must be true, because she was eight and she knew lots of
stuff.

"Well, buddy, I guess it just happened like that. They
must have got crossed up when you were in Mom's belly,"
she said, giving it little thought.

"But *why? Why* did they get crossed up?" he questioned
again.

"I guess that's just how you were made, Char-Char," she
answered. Moments of silence passed in the back seat, while
I held my breath in the front.

"Mommy?" he called out, throwing his little voice to
the Jeep's front. It was a "listen to me" plea, as if I hadn't

225

been waiting on his every breath. "How come my tubes got crossed up, how come?" he asked.

"I'm not sure, buddy. I don't really know how that happened. Things like that just happen to babies sometimes," I said.

"Well, did something like that happen to Sophie when she was a baby? Were her tubes crossed up?" he questioned.

"No, sweet boy," I softly replied. We drove along in silence, letting our thoughts drop where they may. It wasn't the first time he'd asked.

"What are all those things?" Charlie said, breaking our silence once more. He was pointing out his open window at the hundreds of stately headstones tightly packed next to one another beyond the white, cast-iron fence of a grand old cemetery.

"That's where all the dead people are," Sophie said. See, she did know lots of stuff.

"What? Where are they?" he questioned.

"They're buried under the ground, and those big crosses and stuff have their names on them," Sophie said in her "I know stuff" matter-of-fact way. I looked back at him in the rear view mirror. His face was covered in question, eyebrows raised like *Come on, there's no way all those things have dead people under them?!* But Sophie *had* said so. . . . More silence, more processing.

"Mommy, your friend Kelli died because she didn't wear her seat belt, right?" Charlie said, moving on.

"Well, yes, buddy, that's right, she died in a car accident," I answered.

Then, using the Arabic word for "Grandma," Charlie asked, "Mommy, why did Teta Jacqueline die?" His wheels were really turning now.

"She was old, honey, and sick. Remember, she had a disease that made it hard for her to breathe?"

"So are Kelli and Teta Jacqueline buried over there under the ground?" he asked.

"No, hun, they're not buried in this cemetery. There are lots of cemeteries all over in different places. People are usually buried near the city they lived in."

When Charlie learns something of interest, he'll share it in a rather theatrical way. With the white iron fence disappearing in the distance behind us, he extended his hand toward the cemetery and announced, "You see all those dead people, Sophie? You see them? All of those dead people have their heads chopped *off!*" I shook my head reflexively, as if to rattle his sentence loose and knock it out. I was certain I must not have heard him correctly.

"What? No, they don't!" Sophie replied.

"Oh, yes, they do, they totally do! You see, Sophie, when you die, your soul goes to heaven to be with Jesus. But *only*"—great dramatic pause on *only*—"your body stays here. So, your head gets, well . . . chopped off." He said it dramatically, making a cutting motion with his hand across his neck.

Conversations rushed back to me, and now they made perfect sense. Charlie had repeatedly asked me what happens to you after you die, and each time I'd tell him, he'd look at me with the most bewildered expressions. Repeatedly I'd said to him, "*Just* your body stays here, but the you that makes you *you*, that place in your heart called your soul, it goes to heaven to be with Jesus."

And so, we spent the remainder of our sunny drive discussing how you actually don't get your head chopped off after you die. Hard as I tried, I couldn't steer the conversation away from headless corpses. I was forced to admit that there was the possibility that somebody buried in that cemetery died because their head was chopped off, and they, in fact, would be buried without their head attached.

Crossed-up tubes, headstones, and headless bodies—you can't prepare for this; I was just along for the ride.

Shine On

Spring 2012

> *. . . because of the tender mercy of our God, by which the rising sun will come to us from heaven to shine on those living in darkness and in the shadow of death, to guide our feet into the path of peace. —Luke 1:78-79 (New International Version)*

The doorbell rang, and a mad rush for shoes and backpacks ensued. Charlie had developed a bit of his big sister's sense of non-urgency, so I'd taken the creative tack of relying on our ten-year-old neighbor girl to help get the kids to the bus stop on time. It was the same story each morning: Amber would ring our bell at 8:55, sending our puppy into a frenzy of barking and whimpering. Tucker knew the kids would be leaving on the bus, so he would start his daily tantrum at the front door, begging to have his leash on, hoping he'd be able to see them off.

This particular day, Amber came into the entryway, bouncy and chatty as ever. She was as blonde as Sophie was dark. Cute, trendy pink glasses frames surrounded her baby-blue eyes. Some days she spent all her breath telling Tucker how weird he was for freaking out every morning. Some days it was chatter about what was going on at school. More often than not, she talked about what was going on at her house. Her energy for early-morning gab made me smile.

What I've come to recognize, since having Charlie, is that everyone has a story. Some pivotal thing happens in each of our lives—something that we hang on for, something we work through. Perhaps we allow God to pick us up in our exhaustion and carry us through it. For example, Amber and her little brother had come to know their new mom and dad only four years ago. The state had scooped them out of their neglectful home and placed them up for adoption. Their shiny new parents had struggled with years of infertility, longing for a family. Holding onto one another, they took a leap of faith. They opened their home and their hearts. The ride was a bit bumpy, but now they had a girl and a boy who called them Mom and Dad. Story made.

Amber chattered away as we ran around the house shoving homework and snacks into backpacks. Sophie was ready, so I sent her out the front door with Amber. Charlie insisted on walking Tucker to the bus stop *all by himself*. He struggled to get our frantic pup to stay still long enough to get his leash clasped to his harness. Out the front door we went, trailing behind the girls. The storm door slammed behind us, and sunlight bounced from the glass.

Looking forward, I saw my girl, confident, beautiful, and independent. She never looked back. I was proud of the young lady she'd become. She journeyed ahead, and a piece of my heart went always with her, even if she was unaware of it.

The morning air was brisk and fresh, the start of a perfect spring day. "Slow down, dog, you're gonna puke!" Charlie yelled out to Tucker. Tucker looked like a teeny pack dog pulling an overloaded sled. Trying to charge ahead, his back arched and front paws mostly in the air, Tucker strained against the resistance of his harness. Charlie and I looked at each other and giggled.

Charlie's hair was kindergarten-boy wild. His SpongeBob backpack bounced off one shoulder. He struggled to keep up with our ten-pound, oatmeal-colored, big-eared mass of energy. "I love you, Charlie," I said.

"I love you too, Mom," he replied, bouncing along.

"Charlie, I'm so glad I got you. Of all the little boys in the world, I'm so happy that you're the one I got, 'cause you're the best one," I said.

"You think I'm the best boy?" he questioned.

"Yes, I do," I said.

With a wide grin, he said, "Yeah, if you would've got another one, he'd probably stink!"

With the bus coming in the distance, Charlie and Tucker ran ahead to join the circle of kids at the corner. Tucker promptly flopped over onto his back for his morning belly rub from the neighbor kids. The bus approached and I took over the leash. I watched my girl and boy climb the wide stairs with the others. The driver smiled and waved at me. She pulled the mechanical lever toward her, closing the accordion door. They pulled away and disappeared up and over the hilltop. Tucker looked up at me with sad eyes. His morning excitement dissipated with the bus's exhaust.

I walked toward home. Sunlight streamed down through the trees above. I thought about this place of peace that God had led me to. After my time spent gathered up in his arms, he had gently set me down, and for now, he walked beside me. The day was fresh and new. This wasn't the life I had planned for; incredibly, it was so much more.

Reflections

*I*t is in my sorrow that I most easily see the face of God. He is with me; I've seen him bear witness to my brokenness. He has been etched within me while I lay in darkness. He lifts me up in my despair. In his strength, I move forward once more. Now that I've known him in the dark, I see him in the light with an ease I hadn't before. His face is undeniable both in the light of day and in the darkest of nights. I've been embraced.

A place for Gratitude

To my amazingly supportive, loving family: You're the best! Paul, thank you for believing in me, always. To Sophie and Charlie, thank you for letting me be your Mama.

To Jeff and Melissa, Doug and Brooke: Thank you for allowing me to share your sons' stories.

To the rest of my family and friends: Thank you for your relentless encouragement. I'm one blessed girl!

To Dr. Amarjit Singh: The dedication you had to your work, and the many lives you enriched, will never be forgotten. Thank you for taking care of our family.

To Dr. Francis Moga and the rest at The Children's Heart Clinic, Minneapolis, Minnesota: Again, with the ridiculously insignificant "Thank You!" www.childrensheartclinic.org

To Children's Hospital in Minneapolis—especially the NICU, PICU, and Cardiac Floor nurses: Thank you for your exceptional, top-notch care and commitment to our kids. www.childrensmn.org

To Heidi Mann: Thank you for helping me frame my creative ramblings into a prettier picture. You've been the best! www.FinalTouchProofreadingAndEditing.com

To our heart family at Camp Odayin: Thanks for loving our kids and teaching all of us: "You can be happy if you let yourself be." www.campodayin.org

To baby Zachariah and our beautiful Kelli: I'll choose to think of you in each other's arms, until we meet again. Godspeed.

Glossary

*E*xcept where noted, definitions are from *Merriam-Webster Medical Dictionary*, at http://unabridged.merriam-webster.com/. All websites listed here were accessed June 6, 2014.

aorta: the large arterial trunk that carries blood from the heart to be distributed by branch arteries through the body

cardiopulmonary bypass machine (sometimes referred to as "heart-lung bypass machine" or simply "bypass"): a machine that takes over the heart's pumping action and moves blood away from the heart during surgery, allowing the surgeon to operate on a heart that isn't beating and that doesn't have blood flowing through it *(adapted from text at the National Heart, Lung, and Blood Institute website, http://www.nhlbi.nih.gov/health/health-topics/topics/hs/during.html)*

CaringBridge: a nonprofit offering protected websites to connect people during health crises; serving more than 500,000 people each day *(adapted from text at http://www.caringbridge.org)*

coarctation: a stricture or narrowing especially of a canal or vessel (as the aorta)

coronary artery: either of two arteries that arise one from the left and one from the right side of the aorta immediately above the semilunar valves and supply the tissues of the heart itself

echocardiogram (abbreviated "EKG"): a visual record made by echocardiography; *also*: the procedure for producing such a record

hypoplastic left heart: a congenital malformation of the heart in which the left side is underdeveloped resulting in insufficient blood flow

intensivist: a physician who specializes in the care and treatment of patients in intensive care

neonatologist: a specialist in neonatology, a branch of medicine concerned with the care, development, and diseases of newborn infants

NICU (Neonatal Intensive Care Unit): a nursery in a hospital that provides around-the-clock care to sick or premature babies *(http://www.marchofdimes.com/baby/in-the-nicu.aspx)*

perinatology: a branch of medicine concerned with care of high-risk pregnancies *(http://www.fetalcare.org/glossary-of-terms)*

PICU (Pediatric Intensive Care Unit): an area within a hospital specializing in the care of critically ill infants, children, and teenagers *(http://en.wikipedia.org/wiki/Pediatric_intensive_care_unit)*

pulmonary artery: an arterial trunk or either of its two main branches that carry oxygen-deficient blood to the lungs

septal wall (or "septum"): a dividing wall or membrane especially between bodily spaces or masses of soft tissue

septostomy: the surgical creation of an opening through the interatrial septum; **interatrial:** situated between the atria of the heart; **atrium (singular of "atria"):** a chamber of the heart that receives blood from the veins and forces it into a ventricle or ventricles; **ventricle:** a chamber of the heart which receives blood from a corresponding atrium and from which blood is forced into the arteries

tachycardia: relatively rapid heart action whether physiological (as after exercise) or pathological

Transposition (of the Great Arteries): the displacement of a viscus to a side opposite from that which it normally occupies; **viscus:** an internal organ of the body, especially one (as the heart, liver, or intestine) located in the large cavity of the trunk

triple test (also called "triple screen," "Kettering test," "Bart's test"): a blood test for pregnant women for alpha-fetoprotein, human chorionic gonadotropin, and estriol in order to assess the risk of fetal abnormality

ventilator (also called a "respirator"): a device for maintaining artificial respiration

Made in the USA
San Bernardino, CA
13 February 2015